W9-CON-261

Betty Crocker's

Best Recipes of the Year

Betty Crocker's

Best Recipes of the Year

PRENTICE HALL

New York London Toronto Sydney Tokyo

Prentice Hall
15 Columbus Circle
New York, New York 10023

Library of Congress Cataloging-in-Publication Data

Crocker, Betty.
[Recipes of the year]
Betty Crocker's recipes of the year.—1st ed.
p. cm.
Includes index.
ISBN 0-13-073560-4
1. Cookery.
I. Title. II. Title: Recipes of the year.
TX714.C76 1989 89–8422
641.5—dc20 CIP

Manufactured in the United States of America

10 9 8 7 6 5 4 3 2 1

First Edition

Cover photograph by Anthony Johnson

Cover: Chicken with Figs in Port Sauce (page 66)

Frontispiece: Turkey Tamale Pie (page 78)

Quality Printing and Binding by
The Lakeside Press
R.R. Donnelley & Sons Company
Willard Manufacturing Division
1145 Conwell Avenue
Willard, Ohio 44888-9462
U.S.A.

Contents

Introduction

It was a great year for food. New ingredients, new technology and new ideas popped up at every turn. We've harvested the best Betty Crocker recipes; they represent the lively, health-oriented, wonderfully seasoned food that is what's new in American cooking. Just for the fun of it, we've included a quick look at the year's newsmakers, from "hypermarkets" with acres of selling space to an update on health helps like olive oil and oat bran, to kids who cook real meals.

Our recipes derive their inspiration from every corner of this country and from as far away as Indonesia and the Middle East. Hitherto unheard-of vegetables such as lemon grass become a flavorful addition to a smooth rice side dish; new approaches to old favorites include fettuccine flavored with chipotle chiles. The return to down-home foods is reflected in substantial Company Pot Roast and roast chicken with a hearty oat stuffing. This year's best food is diverse; it's grilled and microwaved, simmered, poached and fried. While a salad offers a stylish quick and easy meal, pasta remains a culinary star. Our selection of more than two hundred imaginative recipes shows you just what's happening in the world of food.

THE BETTY CROCKER EDITORS

TRENDS, TRENDS, TRENDS, TRENDS

By 1993, two-thirds of all American women will be working outside the home. What does this mean for the future of the family dinner? If we use today's statistics as a guide to the crystal ball, we'll see a shimmering image of high-tech help for cooks, more take-out dinners, quick but healthy meals, new foods and new uses for old ones and kids in the kitchen doing a lot more than drying the dishes.

WHAT'S IN STORE?

New technology enables today's supermarkets to offer more and more different foods. The number of vegetable varieties in any good produce department is suddenly nothing short of mind-boggling; fish never seen in U.S. waters find themselves for sale in Phoenix; vegetables that don't grow here in January—or don't grow here at all—are more and more available, all thanks to advances in air freight and refrigeration.

Supermarkets are getting not only better but bigger as well. A European brainstorm, known here as the "hypermarket," has been transported from France to Philadelphia, Cincinnati and a number of other all-American cities. Averaging 150,000 to 200,000 square feet, more than four times the size of the run-of-the-mill market, hypermarkets offer everything from tires to dry-cleaning services, in addition to more food than you've ever seen under one roof. These stores are so big that price checkers wheel around on roller skates, handicapped and elderly shoppers are offered motorized shopping carts, and more than sixty cash registers ring up sales for seven acres of store.

Today's supermarkets will often do the cooking for you—sales of prepared food are up 260 percent over the past fifteen years—or they'll teach you how to cook by computer. The Cuisine Screen, in more than one hundred markets coast to coast, provides serving and cooking tips at the touch of its screen. Need nutritional information or a selection of recipes? Want to learn how to bone a chicken? Just touch the screen.

Hands-on becomes hands-off, too. Honest-to-goodness robots are in the process of replacing your friendly checkout clerk and his chatty cash register, too. Day or night, you'll be able to check yourself out with Checkrobot. No waiting, no conversation. But will it give you an insulated bag for the ice cream? Unfortunately, nobody's figured out how to get groceries into bags without human help, so you may have to do it yourself.

CARRY-OUT CARRIES ON

The lifestyle equation for today might be this: 2 incomes = ½ the time at home, especially time in the kitchen. And so, with more and more women working outside the home, less and less time is spent at the stove. According to a recent survey by a national magazine, 61 percent of those sampled buy fancy take-out food. In an effort to spend more time with their children, modern moms are picking up restaurant food after work and serving it in the comfort of their own homes—probably after zapping it in the microwave to reheat. Take-out dinners have increased 50 percent since 1984 and more and more restaurants are offering them. A famed restaurant in San Francisco has added a fish-and-chips-to-go counter where you can also split with a split of champagne. And, an editor of a restaurant magazine predicts that by 1991, one out of four restaurant meals will be eaten at home. Baby boomers want to be home with their own babies, but they often don't have time to cook.

THE SEARCH FOR FLAVOR INTENSIFIES

The dilemma is, with no time to cook, we're still on the lookout for food that tastes good. More and more Americans are growing adventurous, at least in regard to our willingness to try new flavors. Perhaps this is because we spend too much time at work and we're looking for excitement wherever we can find it—even in the food we eat. Hot imports from Mexico, China and Thailand are having a breathtaking effect on our appetites. Chile fever is fanned by our native Southwest fare, and it increasingly carries over from the local taco stand to the home kitchen. Exotic ingredients are more available but may still be confusing. If you don't know the difference between a *poblano* and a *pasilla*, check out our glossary.

The Hot Stuff

A Glossary of Chiles

Chiles are native to the Americas. They have been known in North America for some time but are said to have traveled north by a circuitous route; apparently they found their way from Mexico to the Western world with Christopher Columbus, then to the East and finally back to North America. New strains of chiles are developed frequently, bred for hardiness, sweetness, hotness and so forth. But chiles are full of surprises; two chiles picked from the same plant may vary wildly in hotness. To quench the fire of a too-spicy mouthful, do not reach for a water glass. Water will only spread the capsaicin (the compound that our tongues register as "hot") around. Instead, take a large mouthful of something starchy: corn chips, beans, bread or rice. Sometimes finding fresh chiles is difficult. This probably isn't a question of distribution, but of perishability. Canned and dried chiles are usually available.

ANAHEIM CHILES *(California green chiles) are slim, between five and eight inches long and of various light shades of green. These mildly hot chiles are sometimes twisted in appearance. They are occasionally stuffed, but their flesh is thin and more fragile than that of poblano chiles. The Anaheims cultivated in New Mexico—where the name is* chile verde*—are reputedly hotter. A ripe, red Anaheim is sometimes known as a* chile Colorado*. Anaheim chiles are dried and tied in wreaths* (ristras)*, and ground and blended in commercial chili powder mixtures. They may be purchased in cans as "mild green chiles." These chiles were named after the town that, at the turn of the century, was the site of a chile cannery.*

ANCHO *refers to a ripened, dried poblano chile.*

CASCABEL CHILES, *true ones, are scarcer than hen's teeth in most parts of the United States. Sometimes dried Anaheim chiles are labeled "cascabel," but they are very different from the authentic item. Fresh cascabel chiles are hot and have a distinctive flavor. They are round, and 1½ inches in diameter. Dried, the cascabel chile has a nutlike flavor.*

CAYENNE CHILES *are thin and tapered, three to seven inches long. Dark green (unripe) or bright red (ripe), the cayenne is incendiary and well known to Asian kitchens. The red ones are dried and ground to make cayenne pepper (here, "ground red pepper"). This product adds heat and just a little chile flavor.*

CHILI POWDER *This is a mixture of ground, dried red chiles blended with other spices and herbs. It is said to have been invented by Willie Gebhardt, a Texan, in 1892. Most brands include cumin and oregano. Often chili powder formulas contain paprika, coriander and salt. Chili powder is not to be confused with ground red chiles.*

CHIPOTLE CHILES *are smoked, dried jalapeños with a very wrinkled appearance. Fresh jalapeños are vibrant green but they turn brown when smoked. Chipotles can be purchased loose (dry) or canned in adobo sauce. The canned variety is convenient as it saves having to soak and soften them.*

GUAJILLO CHILES (MIRASOL CHILES) *have a vegetal flavor that shines even through the drying process. Guajillos are orange-red, skinny and about two to three inches long.*

JALAPEÑO CHILES *range from hot to very hot. They are dark green, fat and about two to three inches long with a characteristically rounded tip. Watch out for the little ones, which are hottest. Jalapeños ripen to red. Use them fresh or pickled.*

PASILLA CHILES *are hot and brown (almost black when dried, which is how they are commonly found). They have a dusky flavor.*

POBLANO *is the chile most frequently used for* chiles rellenos. *It is a suave dark green and ranges from mild to hot. Shaped like a long bell pepper, the poblano has a nice shape for stuffing.*

RED PEPPER FLAKES *are just that: flaked, dried ripe chiles. Most red pepper flake mixtures are quite hot.*

SERRANO CHILES *are a sort of middling green, developing to brilliant red when ripe. Extremely hot (as hot as any chile), the chile is usually shorter and thinner than the jalapeño.*

CHILE SAFETY

The flesh, ribs and seeds of chiles are rich in irritating, burning oils. When preparing chiles, always wash hands and utensils in soapy water. Be especially careful not to rub your face—eyes in particular—until the oils have been thoroughly washed away. When processing chiles in a blender or food processor, avert your face as even the fumes are burning. Some cooks who work with chiles for any extended length of time wear plastic gloves. There is a higher concentration of capsaicin in the ribs of chiles; remove them for a milder chile.

ROASTING CHILES

Recipes often call for chiles to be roasted. This enhances the flavor and makes them a snap to peel. Roasted chiles may be frozen before peeling, a convenience if you roast a big batch at once; wrap them airtight in plastic wrap.

BROILER METHOD

Set oven control to broil. Arrange whole chiles with their top surfaces about 5 inches from the heat. (Some people cut a small slit in the shoulder of each chile, to prevent it from bursting.) Broil, turning occasionally, until the skin is blistered and evenly browned (not burned). Remove to a plastic bag and close tightly; let chiles sit for 20 minutes, then peel. Anaheim and poblano chiles roast in 12 to 17 minutes; jalapeño and serrano chiles, in 5 minutes.

GAS STOVE-TOP METHOD

Spear a whole chile on a long-handled metal fork and hold it about 5 inches from the flame. Turn the chile so that it roasts evenly. Place roasted chiles in a plastic bag and close tightly; let chiles sit for 20 minutes, then peel. The disadvantage to this method is that you can't roast a number of chiles at once.

ELECTRIC STOVE-TOP METHOD

This involves a little ingenuity on the part of the cook. Arrange a sturdy, heatproof metal rack (such as a cake rack) so that the grill sits about 4 to 5 inches above the electric burner. Place whole chiles on the rack over high heat. Turn the chiles occasionally so that they roast evenly. Remove chiles to a plastic bag and close tightly; let chiles sit for 20 minutes, then peel.

Fanciful Fruit

Culinary horizons are expanding to include a panoply of previously unfamiliar fruits and vegetables, and fish unknown in local waters. Orange roughy is hardly a household word in most of the United States; it's just one type of imported fish that fish markets are selling to keep pace with the ever-increasing American appetite for seafood. Nutrition and flavor are both responsible for this finny favoritism. Luckily, using the microwave is among the best and most healthful ways to cook fish. Believe it or not, deer and buffalo are becoming more at home on the range, too.

The produce department of most markets has turned into an intriguing display of exotics like cherimoya, Asian pears, tomatillos and tamarillos that you'll bet are really tasty if only you knew what to do with them.

Help yourself to How to Use the New Produce on page 7.

Just for the Health of It

If you can never become too rich or too thin, why are Americans driving themselves crazy trying? We definitely seem to be working harder and a lot more of us are working—presumably to attain "the good life." We've become so health- and weight-conscious, we're breeding leaner cattle and pigs, drinking more skim milk and a lot less alcohol. The American Heart Association is currently identifying products it deems to be heart-healthy. Special stickers will soon adorn the packages of processed foods that qualify.

We're lapping up olive oil as if it were the cure for everything including the common cold. While not really a cure-all, this new food hero is truly good for you. Here's why: Olive oil, like any other plant product, has no cholesterol of its own. As a monounsaturate, it lowers the level of low-density lipoprotein cholesterol without lowering the "good-guy" type, the high-density lipoprotein cholesterol. It tastes good, too. (It is also high in calories, even a little higher than butter.) Its healthy characteristics, combined with its sunny intense flavor, have helped olive oil attain a level of acceptance in the United States that may soon rival its age-old popularity in the Mediterranean where, maybe not so coincidentally, the rate of heart attacks is lower than anywhere else in the Western world. For many, it also makes the best salad dressing in the world, bar none.

HOW TO USE THE NEW PRODUCE

PRODUCE	CHOOSE	USE
Arugula	*Small dark-green leaves; crisp stems*	*Adds bitter tang to salads, soups.*
Asian pear	*Firm, yellow, freckled, fragrant*	*Slice and eat, or use in desserts as you would any pear; stays crisp even after cooking.*
Carambola	*Waxy skin; green is tart, yellow is sweet; both lemony in flavor*	*Do not peel. Just slice for tart-flavored, star-shaped garnish for fish, vegetables or fruit.*
Cherimoya	*Grayish green; slightly soft to the touch*	*Split in half, remove seeds and eat with spoon as a melon. Soft, creamy, sweet.*
Coriander (also called cilantro)	*Dark green leaves that are neither yellow nor limp; crisp stems*	*Seasoning for Mexican, Southwest or Chinese cuisines.*
Gingerroot	*Firm, knobby, not wrinkled*	*Mince and use in Chinese recipes.*
Jicama	*Firm, large, not wrinkled or spongy*	*Peel and dice for crisp, water chestnutlike texture.*
Kiwifruit	*Brown and fuzzy, soft to the touch*	*Peel and slice in fruit cup or as garnish.*
Lemon grass	*Smooth, firm*	*Peel and cook. A staple of Thai cooking; not so sour as lemon.*
Mango	*Smooth, plump, fragrant; leathery skin inedible*	*Peel and dice for fruit cups, salads, sorbets. Cook when using in chutney.*
Papaya	*Green or yellow to orange*	*Use green as you might squash—halve and grill or broil. Use yellow as you might melon.*
Radicchio	*Crisp, tight, small heads*	*Adds color and texture to salads. Braising or simmering intensifies flavor.*
Tamarillo	*Firm, yellow or red; yellow often sweeter*	*Peel and cook in chutney, or serve raw with sugar and lime juice.*
Tomatillo	*Firm, green or yellow; papery husk intact*	*Remove husks and use raw or cooked in salsas or as a side dish.*

Where There's Smoke

The cookout grill, known in much of the nation as the barbecue, is second only to the microwave oven in growing popularity. It provides a low-fat cooking technique that is also fast and tasty. Who could ask for more? Well, how about even more flavor? These days, where there's smoke there's most likely some fancy wood, too, such as mesquite, hickory, apple or pecan. Take a look at the table below to see what they add.

Where There's Smoke

Woods	Flavor	Heat and Smoke
Alder	*Sweet and delicate*	*Moderate heat and smoke*
Fruit	*Light and lingering*	*Moderate heat; mild smoke*
Hickory	*Strong, pungent, smoky*	*High heat; heavy smoke*
Mesquite	*Strong, sweet, rich, woody*	*High heat; heavy and flavorful smoke. Use 1/3 mesquite to 2/3 charcoal*
Nut	*Sweet and delicate*	*Low heat for slow cooking; minimal smoke*
Oak	*Mellow and fresh*	*Medium heat and smoke*

COLD CEREAL IS HOT!

Led by high-fiber brands and the highly acclaimed oat bran, breakfast cereals have really begun to rise and shine. They broke all-time sales records in 1987, were up 1.1 percent per person in 1988 and will probably double that leap when the figures are totaled for 1989. Oat bran fans are using the grain to make cookies, muffins and bread; they're sprinkling it on salads and gobbling it up in cereals. Find out how much actual soluble fiber (credited with cholesterol-lowering characteristics) and other healthy benefits there are in your favorite food by sending a self-addressed, stamped envelope to the Center for Science in the Public Interest, 1501 16th St., N.W., Washington, D.C. 20036.

Hot cereal is hot, too, with some experts claiming as much as a 20 percent growth spurt over the last year. The microwave oven helps to hurry it along. According to the *Environmental Nutrition Newsletter*, an associate professor of nutrition at Kent State University says that breakfast at home is better for you than a restaurant breakfast—supplying less fat and more vitamins and minerals. So, set your alarm a couple of minutes earlier and get off to a good start at home.

READ LABEL BEFORE EATING

Government agencies make diet and nutrition recommendations. The Surgeon General advises us to lower fat; the National Research Council says to lower salt and increase complex carbohydrates. But, so far their regulations regarding food labeling have been vague at best. The consensus is that food labels should include fat levels, saturated fats, cholesterol, sodium, calories, carbohydrates and fiber. Most experts would like to see the level of calcium and of vitamins A and C as well, but they don't regard the percentages of other vitamins as crucial. Today, only foods that are fortified, or make a health or diet claim, are required to carry nutritional information on their labels. But then it must be complete: serving size, fat, protein and carbohydrate content, percentages of U.S. Recommended Daily Allowances of protein, vitamins A and C, three types of B vitamins, plus calcium and iron.

About 55 percent of FDA-regulated products currently carry nutrition labeling, and food manufacturers are generally in favor of some federal rules, if only to avoid conforming to fifty different standards from fifty states.

THEY'RE NOT JUST KIDDING AROUND

There are about 24 million teenagers on the loose with the opportunity to spend as much as $40 million of their families' hard-earned money—most of it on groceries, according to a recent magazine. Gathering provisions for the family has become one of the chores most likely to be assigned to teenagers whose mothers are working. And the kids are doing a great job, according to a research firm. The young shoppers are making at least half of the brand decisions and they're reading labels to determine nutritional content on a wide variety of foods. Of course, they're also buying a lot of chips and soda.

Plenty of teenagers, and even younger latchkey kids, are helping out with the preparation of meals—or, at least they're feeding themselves. The number of microwave ovens in America's kitchens doubled between 1981 and 1987, and projections show microwaves will be in 90 percent of U.S. homes by the year 2000. About 90 percent of the six- to seventeen-year-olds whose families now own a microwave are allowed, nay encouraged, to operate it. This combination of kids and microwaves has spawned a whole new category of packaged foods. As a balm for busy moms' consciences and a boon for hungry youngsters, several food producers have developed minimicro meals with taste, texture and portion size geared for two- to eight-year-olds. "The aim is nutrition, safety and convenience," said a spokesman for one of the companies.

As of this year, more U.S. households own a microwave than a clock radio.

HYPERDIETERS OR HYPOCRITES?

We may claim to be a nation of dieters, but a National Restaurant Association poll reveals that 65 percent of the restaurateurs surveyed insist that "the richer a dessert is, the better it sells." FIND/SVP, a New York market research company, let the following caloric cat out of the bag: Sales of premium adult desserts (e.g., Dove Bars) may reach $11½ million by the end of 1991. Tsk, tsk. Nobody's perfect.

REGIONAL RIGHTS AND RITES

From coast to coast, and border to border, every area of the country is exulting in its native goods and indigenous style of cooking. Cajun and Creole, the contemporary legends from Louisiana, are now found literally from Maine to California; Southwest influences and ingredients are spreading east and north like wildfire.

Hidebound New England pridefully promotes its Boston baked beans and Rhode Island johnny cakes. It also airmails its clambakes and lobster feasts as far afield as Los Angeles and Seattle.

Seattle boasts an abundance of unique seafood such as the resurgent Olympia oyster, staging a comeback after near-extinction due to water pollution and overharvesting. The Northwest also lays claim to vineyards of cabernet and chardonnay that vie for honors with respected Old World wineries.

California, the original culinary consciousness raiser, with its freshest of produce and most precious of sauces, seems to have peaked in popularity and is even being disowned by bemoaners of tasteless "baby veggies." But the Golden State can rest easily on its bay laurels as having been responsible for starting it all; it's the source of the culinary tremor that has shaken meat-and-potatoes America to its very roots and stimulated an unprecedented interest in food.

Throwing off the yoke of California culinary dominance, two other regions are staking a claim to their right to restaurant recognition. Suddenly the new Old South and the solid Midwest are being acknowledged as food forces.

For years, Midwest restaurateurs were locked in pitched battle with a consumer mentality that said, "I could buy a snow tire for that price," and were forced to offer staid and substantial menus that gave good value—no frills. Even now, some natives are uncomfortable with the term "Midwestern Cuisine." They prefer American Nouvelle and claim their local cookery is still in its evolutionary stages. But seasonal changes and dedicated farmers provide a diversity available in few other regions.

Diversity is a word that crops up often when people talk about Midwestern foods. Iowa pheasant, Indiana persimmons, mushrooms and maple syrup from Michigan, and cheese from Wisconsin are a mere fraction of the total heartland harvest. And with all that good, real food, chefs and diners alike see little need for high falutin' imports or outlandish combinations. In the words of one Midwestern chef, "If there's something you've never seen on a plate before, there's probably a reason." Which is not to imply that the Midwest is stuck in the mud. On the contrary, new restaurants are springing up all over and customers are thronging to them.

The Southern school of cooking concentrates on comfort. From deep in Dixie, crab cakes and fried chicken have been reborn in a low-fat skillet instead of a deep fryer. Light, lower-fat versions of old favorites still use the fresh, flavorful ingredients that made them famous in the first place. Sweet potatoes, pecans and biscuits, biscuits, biscuits say, "Yes, you *can* go home again." Displaced Southerners and sophisticated travelers from all over are ordering down-home foods in restaurants everywhere—and cookin' 'em up at home.

A TV chef in Atlanta describes the cooking of the Nouvelle Confederacy as "quicker, easier and more stylish," but rich and creamy still have their place in Southern (and Yankee) hearts. Sweet potato pie, cornbread, spoon bread and Tennessee pound cake, still made with "a pounda butter and a pounda sugar," satisfy as no health-conscious whole wheat can. In traditional Charleston, shrimp, crab and oysters appear at breakfast, lunch and dinner. The city has recently begun growing its own American tea—on a plantation, of course.

Barbecue is the subject of strident debate among South Carolinians, Texans and Kansans (and a lot of other regional subdivisions). The controversy covers the makeup of the sauce (Is the base tomato, mustard, vinegar or molasses?), the depth and length of the pit, the duration of the cooking process, not to mention the cut and critter to be cooked. Which combination produces the most succulent result? The best way to know for sure is to take a trip. One way to sample some honest-to-goodness regional fare is to participate in some of the hundreds of food festivals held throughout the United States. Try the World Catfish Festival in Belzoni, Mississippi, the Jambalaya Festival in Gonzales, Louisiana, or the Okra Strut in Irmo, South Carolina. Up North, go for the Maple Festival in St. Albans, Vermont, or the Lobster Festival in Winter Harbor, Maine. Here is just a taste of what's out there year-round.

FOOD FESTIVALS

JANUARY

Texas Citrus Fiesta
Box 407
Mission, TX 78572

FEBRUARY

Jalapeño Festival
Jalapeño Festival Committee
2002 Bristol Rd.
Laredo, TX 78041

National Date Festival
(Mid-month)
Indio, CA 92201
(714) 342-8247

Swamp Cabbage Festival
(Last weekend)
LaBelle, FL 33935
(813) 675-0125

MARCH

Maple Harvest Festival
Shaver's Creek Environmental Center
Penn State University
University Park, PA 16802

APRIL

Vermont Maple Festival
(Mid-month)
St. Albans, VT 05478
(802) 524-5800

World Catfish Festival
(Every Saturday)
Belzoni, MS 39038
(601) 247-2616

MAY

Rhubarb Festival
Kitchen Kettle Village
Box 380
Intercourse, PA 17534

National Mushroom Hunting Championship
(Mother's Day Weekend)
Boyne City, MI 49712
(616) 582-6222

JUNE

Jambalaya Festival
(Second weekend)
P.O. Box 1243
Gonzales, LA 70737

National Asparagus Festival
Box 153
Shelby/Hart, MI 49455

Ipswich Strawberry Festival
(Mid-month)
Ipswich, MA 01938
(617) 356-2307

JULY

Pork, Peanut & Pine Festival
(Mid-month)
Chippokes State Park
Surry, VA 23883

Gilroy Garlic Festival
(End of month)
P.O. Box 2311
Gilroy, CA 95020

AUGUST

Indian-style Salmon Bake
(First Sunday)
Sequim Chamber of Commerce
P.O. Box 907
Sequim, WA 98382

Maine Lobster Festival
(Mid-month)
Winter Harbor, ME 04693
(207) 963-2235

SEPTEMBER

Lodi Grape Festival
Graeme Stewart, Festival Manager
Box 848
Lodi, CA 95241

Sorghum and Cider Fair
Billie Creek Village
Box 27
Rockville, IN 47872

Sorghum Sopping Days
(Third weekend)
Waldo, Alabama
Town of Waldo, Route 3
Talladega, AL 35160

OCTOBER

Yambilee
(End of month)
Box 444
Opelousas, LA 70570

Okra-Strut
(First Saturday)
Irmo, SC 29063
(803) 781-7050

NOVEMBER

Louisiana Pecan Festival
(First weekend)
Colfax, LA 71417
(318) 627-3711

Annual Indian Foods Dinner
(Second & third Saturday)
Salamanca, NY 14779
(716) 945-1252

DECEMBER

Bracebridge Dinner
(Christmas Eve, Christmas Day and Christmas Night)
Yosemite National Park, CA 95389
(209) 373-4171

First Things First

Getting off to a good start makes everything go better—including dinner. Whether you choose Cheese Straw Twists (page 21), an Onion Tart (page 17) or cool Santa Fe Melon Soup (page 26), our appetizers won't take long to make and will make your menu all the more delicious for special occasions or simple suppers.

Marinated Gingered Shrimp

THIS IS A SIMPLE JAPANESE PREPARATION THAT CAN BE PRETTILY ARRANGED ON A SERVING PLATE.

1½ pounds frozen shrimp, shelled and deveined
¼ cup soy sauce
3 ounces gingerroot (see page 7), chopped
¼ cup vinegar
2 tablespoons sugar
2 tablespoons sweet sake
1½ teaspoons salt
2 to 3 tablespoons thinly sliced green onion

Cook shrimp as directed on package; drain. Arrange shrimp in single layer in glass or plastic container, 12 x 7½ x 2 inches. Heat soy sauce to boiling; add gingerroot. Reduce heat; simmer uncovered until most of the liquid is absorbed, about 5 minutes. Stir in vinegar, sugar, sake and salt; pour over shrimp. Cover and refrigerate at least 2 hours.

Remove shrimp from marinade with slotted spoon; arrange on serving plate. Garnish with green onion.

60 to 65 shrimp

Chicken Kabobs with Peanut Sauce (page 16) and Marinated Gingered Shrimp

Tex-Mex Peanuts

ADD A LITTLE DESERT HEAT TO A STANDARD COCKTAIL SNACK WITH A SMIDGEON OF CHILI POWDER AND A BIT OF GARLIC.

2 cloves garlic, crushed
1 teaspoon vegetable oil
1 cup unsalted dry-roasted peanuts
1 tablespoon chili powder
½ teaspoon salt

Cook and stir garlic in oil in 8-inch skillet over medium heat until golden brown; discard garlic. Stir peanuts and chile powder into skillet. Cook and stir over medium heat until peanuts are warm, about 2 minutes; drain. Sprinkle with salt.

1 cup peanuts

CHICKEN KABOBS WITH PEANUT SAUCE

EVEN IN THE MOST POLITE SOCIETY, IT SEEMS ACCEPTABLE TO EAT THESE SMALL CHICKEN KABOBS DIRECTLY FROM THE BAMBOO SKEWER. THIS DISH IS SPICY-HOT AND SWEET.

2 large whole chicken breasts (about 2 pounds)
1/4 cup soy sauce
1 tablespoon vegetable oil
1 teaspoon packed brown sugar
1/4 teaspoon ground ginger
1 clove garlic, crushed
Peanut Sauce (below)

Remove bones and skin from chicken breasts. Cut chicken into 3/4-inch pieces. (For ease in cutting, partially freeze chicken.) Mix chicken, soy sauce, oil, brown sugar, ginger and garlic in glass bowl. Cover and refrigerate, stirring occasionally, at least 2 hours.

Prepare Peanut Sauce. Remove chicken from marinade; reserve marinade. Thread 4 or 5 chicken pieces on each of 14 to 16 bamboo skewers. Brush chicken with reserved marinade. Set oven control to broil or 550°. Broil skewers with tops about 4 inches from heat 4 to 5 minutes; turn. Brush with marinade. Broil until chicken is done, 4 to 5 minutes longer. Serve with Peanut Sauce.

About 16 appetizers

PEANUT SAUCE

1 small onion, finely chopped
1 tablespoon vegetable oil
1/3 cup peanut butter
1/3 cup water
1 tablespoon lemon juice
1/4 teaspoon ground coriander
3 to 4 drops red pepper sauce

Cook and stir onion in oil in 1½-quart saucepan until tender. Remove from heat. Stir in remaining ingredients; heat over low heat just until blended (sauce will separate if overcooked).

BLUE CORNMEAL CHICKEN WINGS

BLUE CORNMEAL HAS BECOME A SIGNATURE OF THE NEW SOUTHWEST COOKING; IF YOU CAN'T FIND IT, SUBSTITUTE YELLOW OR WHITE.

1/4 cup lime juice
1/4 cup vegetable oil
1/2 teaspoon crushed red pepper
10 chicken wings (about 2 pounds)
2 tablespoons margarine or butter
1/2 cup blue or yellow cornmeal
2 tablespoons all-purpose flour
1/2 teaspoon salt
1/2 teaspoon ground cumin
1/8 teaspoon pepper

Mix lime juice, oil and red pepper in large glass or plastic bowl. Cut each chicken wing at joints to make 3 pieces; discard tip. Cut off and discard excess skin. Place wings in oil mixture; stir to coat. Cover and refrigerate at least 3 hours, stirring occasionally; drain.

Heat oven to 425°. Heat margarine in rectangular pan, 13 x 9 x 2 inches, in oven until melted. Shake remaining ingredients in plastic bag, or mix in bowl. Shake wings in cornmeal mixture to coat; place in pan. Bake uncovered 20 minutes; turn. Bake until golden brown, 20 to 25 minutes longer.

20 appetizers

ONION TART

THIS RUSTIC FRENCH BREAD FEATURES THE PROVENÇAL TOUCH OF OLIVE OIL AND THE WONDERFUL ANCHOVIES AND CURED OLIVES OF THE MEDITERRANEAN.

1 loaf (16 ounces) frozen bread dough
3 tablespoons olive or vegetable oil
3 large onions, thinly sliced
1 tablespoon snipped fresh basil or thyme leaves
⅛ teaspoon white pepper
2 cans (2 ounces each) anchovy fillets, drained
10 oil-cured Greek olives, cut into halves and pitted

Thaw bread dough as directed on package. Heat oil in 10-inch skillet until hot. Stir in onions; reduce heat. Cover and cook, stirring occasionally, until onions are very tender, about 25 minutes. Stir in basil and white pepper.

Shape dough into flattened rectangle on lightly floured surface. Roll dough with floured rolling pin into rectangle, 14 x 11 inches. Place on lightly greased cookie sheet; let rest 15 minutes.

Spoon onion mixture evenly over dough to within 1 inch of edge. Arrange anchovies in lattice pattern on onions. Top with olives. Let tart rest 15 minutes.

Heat oven to 425°. Bake until crust is brown, 15 to 20 minutes.

8 to 10 servings

HERBED LIVER PÂTÉ

LIKE MANY PÂTÉS, BOTH SMOOTH AND COARSE, HERBED LIVER PÂTÉ IS DELICIOUS SERVED WITH CORNICHONS—TINY, WHOLE PICKLED CUCUMBERS.

1 medium onion, chopped
2 tablespoons margarine or butter
1 pound chicken livers
½ teaspoon salt
½ teaspoon dried thyme leaves
½ teaspoon crushed dried rosemary leaves
½ teaspoon dried marjoram leaves
½ teaspoon ground sage
⅛ teaspoon pepper
2 tablespoons Cognac or Madeira
¼ cup whipping cream
French bread, thinly sliced and toasted

Cook and stir onion in margarine in 10-inch skillet over medium heat until tender. Add livers. Cook over medium-high heat, stirring occasionally, until livers are no longer pink inside, about 12 minutes. Reduce heat to low; stir in salt, thyme, rosemary, marjoram, sage and pepper. Cook and stir 1 minute.

Place liver mixture in food processor workbowl fitted with steel blade. Add Cognac to skillet; stir Cognac, and scrape drippings from skillet. Add to liver mixture. Cover and process with about 15 on/off motions until mixture is very finely chopped. Add whipping cream. Cover and process, adding 2 or 3 teaspoons whipping cream if necessary, until smooth and fluffy, about 15 seconds.

Pack liver mixture into small bowl or crock. Cover and refrigerate at least 6 hours. Let stand at room temperature about 30 minutes before serving. Serve with French bread. Garnish with cornichons and parsley if desired.

1½ cups pâté

FOLLOWING PAGES: Onion Tart, Herbed Liver Pâté and Cheese Straw Twists (page 21)

JADOT
EN 1859
RAN
FRANCE
750 ml
WHITE BURGUNDY
TABLE WINE
IMPORTERS

SMOKED SALMON QUICHE WITH FRESH DILL WEED

Pastry for One-Crust Pie (below)
*¾ to 1 cup flaked smoked salmon**
1 cup shredded Swiss cheese (4 ounces)
2 tablespoons chopped green onion
3 eggs
1¼ cups half-and-half
2 teaspoons snipped fresh dill weed
½ teaspoon salt

Prepare Pastry. Heat oven to 425°. Sprinkle salmon, cheese and onion in pastry-lined quiche dish.

Beat eggs slightly in small bowl; beat in remaining ingredients. Pour into dish. Bake uncovered 15 minutes. Reduce oven temperature to 325°. Bake until knife inserted halfway between center and edge comes out clean, 20 to 25 minutes longer. Let stand 10 minutes before cutting.

4 servings

**1 can (8 ounces) red sockeye salmon or 1 can (6½ ounces) tuna, drained and flaked, can be substituted for the smoked salmon.*

PASTRY FOR ONE-CRUST PIE

1 cup all-purpose flour
½ teaspoon salt
⅓ cup plus 1 tablespoon shortening
2 to 3 tablespoons water

Mix flour and salt; cut in shortening until particles are size of small peas. Sprinkle in water, 1 tablespoon at a time, tossing with fork until all flour is moistened and pastry almost cleans side of bowl (1 to 2 teaspoons water can be added if necessary).

Gather pastry into ball; shape into flattened round on lightly floured cloth-covered board. Roll pastry 1½ inches larger than inverted quiche dish with floured cloth-covered rolling pin. Fold pastry into quarters; place in dish with point in center. Unfold and ease into dish, pressing firmly against bottom and side. Trim overhanging edge of pastry 1 inch from rim of dish. Fold and roll pastry under, even with dish; flute if desired.

BELL PEPPER RAJAS

RAJAS (*"STRIPS"*) *USUALLY REFERS TO RIBBONS OF CHILES.* THESE *PEPPER RAJAS ARE A NACHO-LIKE SNACK IN WHICH PEPPERS REPLACE THE TRADITIONAL CORN CHIPS.*

½ green bell pepper, seeded and cut into 6 strips
½ red bell pepper, seeded and cut into 6 strips
½ yellow bell pepper, seeded and cut into 6 strips
¾ cup shredded Monterey Jack cheese (3 ounces)
2 tablespoons chopped ripe olives
¼ teaspoon crushed red pepper

Cut bell pepper strips crosswise into halves. Arrange in ungreased broilerproof pie pan, 9 x 1¼ inches, or round pan, 9 x 2 inches. Sprinkle with cheese, olives and red pepper.

Set oven control to broil. Broil peppers with tops 3 to 4 inches from heat until cheese is melted, about 3 minutes.

6 servings

TO MICROWAVE: Arrange strips on a microwave-safe serving plate. Sprinkle with toppings and cover loosely with waxed paper. Microwave on high (100%) 1 minute; rotate plate one quarter turn. Microwave 30 to 60 seconds longer, until the cheese has melted.

CHEESE STRAW TWISTS

THE FRENCH HAVE MORE THAN ONE NAME FOR THEIR CHEESE STRAWS. THE TWISTS ARE DIABLOTINS, THE FLAT ONES ARE PAILLETTES (FROM PAILLE, MEANING "STRAW"). THIS RECIPE TAKES ADVANTAGE OF FROZEN PUFF PASTRY, A VERY SATISFACTORY SOLUTION TO THE TIME-CONSUMING PROBLEM OF MAKING PUFF PASTRY AT HOME.

1 package (17¼ ounces) frozen puff pastry
⅔ cup grated Parmesan cheese
1 tablespoon paprika
1 egg, slightly beaten

Thaw pastry as directed on package. Heat oven to 425°. Cover 2 cookie sheets with parchment or heavy brown paper. Mix cheese and paprika. Roll 1 sheet of pastry into rectangle, 10 x 12 inches, on lightly floured surface, using floured stockinet-covered rolling pin.

Brush pastry with egg; sprinkle with 3 tablespoons of the cheese mixture. Gently press cheese mixture into pastry. Turn pastry over; repeat with egg and cheese mixture. Fold pastry lengthwise into halves.

Cut pastry crosswise into ½-inch strips. Unfold strips; roll each end in opposite directions to twist. Place twists on cookie sheet. Bake until twists are puffed and golden brown, 7 to 8 minutes. Repeat with remaining sheet of pastry, egg and cheese mixture.

About 4 dozen twists

CHUNKY TUNA SALSA

HERE IS A WONDERFUL USE FOR THAT MEXICAN STAPLE, PICO DE GALLO, PROBABLY THE BEST-KNOWN SOUTH-OF-THE-BORDER SALSA.

1 can (6½ ounces) tuna, well drained
¾ cup chopped red onion
1 large tomato, chopped
1 jalapeño pepper, seeded and chopped
1 tablespoon lemon juice
Snipped fresh cilantro (see page 7)
Tortilla chips

Break up tuna with fork. Gently mix tuna and remaining ingredients except cilantro and tortilla chips. Sprinkle with cilantro. Serve with tortilla chips.

About 2½ cups salsa

CORN AND WALNUT DIP

GO BEYOND GUACAMOLE WHEN SERVING TORTILLA CHIPS. THIS TANGY, CRUNCHY DIP CAPTURES THE TRUE FLAVOR OF THE SOUTHWEST.

2 packages (8 ounces each) cream cheese, softened
¼ cup vegetable oil
¼ cup lime juice
1 tablespoon ground red chiles
1 tablespoon ground cumin
½ teaspoon salt
Dash of pepper
1 can (8¾ ounces) whole kernel corn, drained
1 cup chopped walnuts
1 small onion, chopped (about ¼ cup)

Beat all ingredients except corn, walnuts and onion in large bowl on medium speed until smooth. Stir in corn, walnuts and onion. Serve with tortilla chips.

4 cups dip

YOGURT CHEESE

IN THE MIDDLE EAST, THIS MILD SPREAD OFTEN MAKES AN APPEARANCE AS A BREAKFAST CHEESE. THE SYRIANS ARE PARTICULARLY KNOWN FOR THEIR FONDNESS FOR YOGURT CHEESE.

4 cups plain yogurt
1 teaspoon salt
Pocket bread, split, cut into wedges and toasted

Line a strainer with double-thickness cheesecloth. Place strainer over bowl. Mix yogurt and salt; pour into strainer. Cover and refrigerate at least 12 hours. Unmold onto plate. Garnish with snipped parsley, Moroccan Herbed Olives (right) or Greek olives if desired. Serve with pocket bread.

About 1½ cups

MOROCCAN HERBED OLIVES

MARINATED OLIVES ARE ESSENTIAL TO A MEZZE OR MAZZA, THE MIDDLE EASTERN COUNTERPART OF AN ITALIAN ANTIPASTO.

1 pound Kalamata or Greek olives
¼ cup olive or vegetable oil
2 tablespoons snipped parsley
2 tablespoons snipped fresh cilantro (see page 7)
1 tablespoon lemon juice
½ teaspoon crushed red pepper
2 cloves garlic, finely chopped

Rinse olives under running cold water; drain. Place in 1-quart jar with tight-fitting lid. Mix remaining ingredients; pour over olives. Cover tightly and refrigerate, turning jar upside down occasionally, 1 to 2 weeks. Serve at room temperature.

About 75 olives

Yogurt Cheese and Moroccan Herbed Olives

DOUBLE CHEESE WHEEL

ARTICHOKE HEARTS AND BASIL ADD UNEXPECTED FLAVORS TO A MELLOW CHEESE SPREAD; PINE NUTS PROVIDE A SUBTLE TEXTURE CHANGE.

1 whole, firm round Chihuahua cheese or Monterey Jack cheese (1 pound)
1 package (3 ounces) cream cheese, softened
¼ cup chopped marinated artichoke hearts, drained
¼ cup pine nuts, toasted (see To Toast, right)
1½ teaspoons snipped fresh basil or ½ teaspoon dried basil leaves

Remove any wax coating or rind from Chihuahua cheese. Hollow out cheese with knife or spoon, leaving a shell ½-inch thick on side and bottom; reserve cheese shell. Finely chop enough of the scooped-out cheese to measure 1 cup (reserve any extra for another use).

Place 1 cup chopped cheese, the cream cheese, artichoke hearts, 3 tablespoons of the pine nuts and the basil in food processor workbowl fitted with steel blade; cover and process until well mixed.

Pack mixture into cheese shell. Sprinkle with remaining 1 tablespoon pine nuts; press lightly. Cover and refrigerate until filling is firm, about 3 hours.

Cut into thin wedges. Serve with assorted crackers if desired.

24 servings

Double Cheese Wheel

TO TOAST

Toasting enhances the flavor of pumpkin seeds and nuts. To toast, spread them in a single layer in an ungreased pan; bake at 350°, stirring and checking for doneness frequently. Nuts are toasted when they are lightly browned. Let almonds, pecans and walnuts bake for 7 to 12 minutes. Pumpkin seeds may take up to 15 minutes. Pine nuts toast more rapidly, in 5 to 7 minutes.

To grind nuts, place ⅓ to ½ cup at a time in the workbowl of a food processor or blender. Process them in short pulses just until ground (longer, and you will have nut butter).

COLD YOGURT-CUCUMBER SOUP

NOTHING IS MORE REFRESHING ON A HOT SUMMER'S DAY THAN THIS MIDDLE EASTERN FAVORITE, A COOL MIXTURE OF FRESH CUCUMBERS AND TANGY YOGURT. IT IS THE PERFECT MAKE-AHEAD APPETIZER FOR SULTRY WEATHER.

2 medium cucumbers
1½ cups plain yogurt
½ teaspoon salt
¼ teaspoon dried mint flakes
⅛ teaspoon white pepper

Cut 7 thin slices from 1 cucumber; reserve. Cut all remaining cucumber into ¾-inch chunks. Place half the cucumber chunks and ¼ cup of the yogurt in blender container. Cover and blend on high speed until smooth.

Add remaining cucumber chunks, the salt, mint and white pepper. Cover and blend until smooth. Add remaining yogurt; cover and blend on low speed until smooth. Cover and refrigerate at least 1 hour. Garnish with reserved cucumber slices.

7 servings (about ½ cup each)

SANTA FE MELON SOUP

A SMOOTH, COOL SOUP REFRESHES THE PALATE BEFORE A SPICY MAIN COURSE—OR, SURPRISINGLY, AFTER.

1 large cantaloupe (about 4 pounds), pared, seeded and chopped
3 tablespoons sugar
2 tablespoons snipped fresh mint leaves
½ cup sour cream
¼ cup dry white wine
2 teaspoons grated orange peel
Fresh mint leaves

Place cantaloupe, sugar and 2 tablespoons mint in food processor workbowl fitted with steel blade or in blender container; cover and process until smooth. Stir in sour cream, wine and orange peel. Garnish with mint leaves.

6 servings (about ⅔ cup each)

Santa Fe Melon Soup

Crumpets (page 137) and Creamy Stilton Soup

Creamy Stilton Soup

Here is a rich and satisfying cheese soup. Stilton cheese is the great English blue-veined cheese that ages to an ivory-pale gold perfection.

½ cup finely chopped onion
½ cup finely chopped carrot
1 bay leaf
¼ cup margarine or butter
¼ cup all-purpose flour
¼ teaspoon white pepper
2 cups chicken broth
1½ cups half-and-half
1½ cups crumbled Stilton cheese (6 ounces)
Snipped parsley

Cook onion, carrot and bay leaf in margarine in 3-quart saucepan until onion and carrot are tender, about 5 minutes. Stir in flour and white pepper. Cook over low heat, stirring constantly until smooth and bubbly; remove from heat. Stir in broth and half-and-half. Heat to boiling over medium heat, stirring constantly; boil and stir 1 minute. Stir in cheese; heat over low heat, stirring constantly, just until cheese is melted. Remove bay leaf; sprinkle soup with parsley.

6 servings

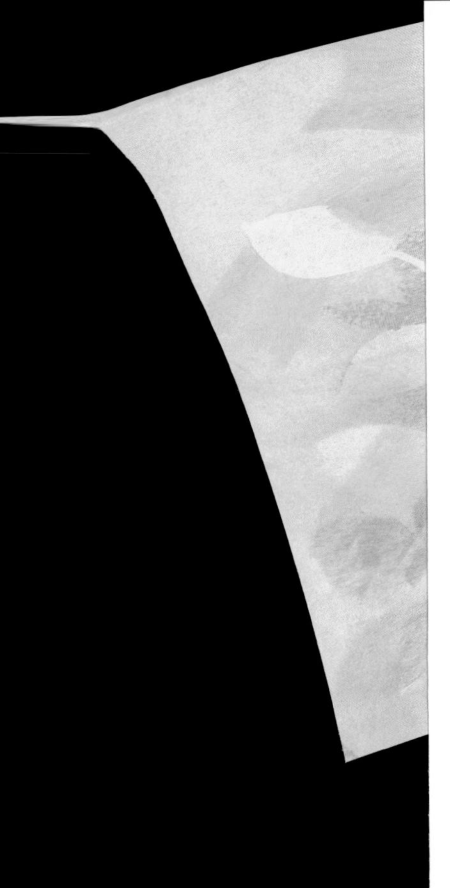

CREAMY FISH SOUP WITH GARLIC TOAST

1½ cups mayonnaise or salad dressing
3 cloves garlic, finely chopped
¼ cup margarine or butter
8 slices French bread
1 clove garlic, cut into halves
1 pound fish fillets, cut into 1-inch pieces
1½ cups chardonnay or dry white wine
¼ teaspoon salt
6 slices onion
3 slices lemon
5 sprigs parsley
1 bay leaf
Paprika

Mix mayonnaise and chopped garlic; cover and refrigerate. Heat 2 tablespoons of the margarine in 10-inch skillet over medium heat until melted. Cook 4 of the bread slices in margarine, turning once, until brown; rub one side of toasted bread with half-clove garlic. Repeat with remaining margarine and bread.

Place fish fillet pieces in same skillet. Add remaining ingredients except paprika; if necessary, add just enough water to cover fish. Heat to boiling; reduce heat. Simmer uncovered until fish flakes easily with fork, about 6 minutes. Remove fish, using slotted spoon; keep warm.

Strain cooking liquid; return to skillet. Gradually beat in mayonnaise mixture, using wire whisk or spoon. Cook over low heat, stirring constantly, until hot and slightly thickened. Fold in fish. Place 2 slices garlic toast upright in each of 4 soup bowls. Pour soup between slices; sprinkle with paprika.

4 servings

TURKEY AND WILD RICE SOUP

SERVE SMALL PORTIONS OF THIS SOUP AS A FIRST COURSE; A LARGER BOWL CAN BE A MEAL IN ITSELF WITH CRUSTY BREAD AND TOSSED SALAD.

½ cup uncooked wild rice
3½ cups water
1 tablespoon instant chicken bouillon (dry)
2 turkey drumsticks (about 1½ pounds)
2 medium stalks celery (with leaves), sliced
1 medium onion, chopped
2 bay leaves
1 can (16 ounces) stewed tomatoes

Mix all ingredients in Dutch oven. Heat to boiling; reduce heat. Cover and simmer until turkey is done and wild rice is tender, 50 to 60 minutes.

Remove turkey drumsticks; cool about 5 minutes. Remove skin and bones from turkey; cut turkey into bite-size pieces. Stir turkey into soup. Heat until hot. Remove bay leaves.

6 servings

TO MICROWAVE: Decrease water to 3 cups and use hot water. Mix all ingredients in 3-quart microwavable casserole. Cover tightly and microwave on high (100%), turning drumsticks over every 10 minutes, until turkey is done, 30 to 40 minutes. Remove turkey; cool about 5 minutes.

Cover wild rice mixture tightly and microwave until wild rice is tender, 8 to 10 minutes longer. Remove skin and bones from turkey; cut turkey into bite-size pieces. Stir turkey into soup. Cover tightly and microwave until hot, 2 to 3 minutes. Remove bay leaves.

Southwestern Bean Soup with Chiles

The mild beans and mellow cheese get a kick from green chiles, chile powder and coriander.

1 medium onion, sliced
1 large clove garlic, crushed
2 tablespoons margarine or butter
1 can (28 ounces) whole tomatoes, undrained
1 can (20 ounces) kidney beans, drained
1 can (16 ounces) pinto beans, drained
1 can (4 ounces) chopped green chiles, drained
1 tablespoon chili powder
¼ teaspoon ground coriander
½ cup shredded Cheddar cheese (2 ounces)
1 cup shredded Monterey Jack cheese (4 ounces)

Cook and stir onion and garlic in margarine in 3-quart saucepan over medium heat until onion is tender, about 5 minutes. Stir in remaining ingredients except cheeses; break up tomatoes. Heat to boiling; reduce heat. Cover and simmer 30 minutes.

Stir in Cheddar cheese and ½ cup of the Monterey Jack cheese; heat over low heat, stirring occasionally, just until cheese is melted. Sprinkle each serving with remaining Monterey Jack cheese.

6 servings

To Microwave: Place onion, garlic and margarine in 3-quart microwavable casserole. Cover tightly and microwave on high (100%) until onion is tender, 2 to 4 minutes. Stir in remaining ingredients except cheeses; break up tomatoes. Cover tightly and microwave 10 minutes; stir.

Cover tightly and microwave until hot and bubbly, 6 to 9 minutes longer. Stir in Cheddar cheese and ½ cup of the Monterey Jack cheese. Cover tightly and let stand until cheese is melted, about 5 minutes. Sprinkle each serving with remaining Monterey Jack cheese.

L

¾ cup
½ cup
6 cups
½ teasp
½ teasp
¼ teasp
½ pack
(1 en
3 ounce
1 cup,
2 tablespoons snipped cilantro (see page 7) or parsley
3 tablespoons lemon juice

Heat lentils, rice, water, cumin, salt, pepper and soup mix (dry) to boiling in Dutch oven; reduce heat. Cover and simmer, stirring occasionally, until lentils and rice are tender, about 40 minutes.

Stir in spinach, cilantro and lemon juice until spinach is wilted. Serve with additional snipped cilantro and lemon slices if desired.

4 servings

Lentil and Brown Rice Soup

White Bean Chili

1 large onion, chopped (about 1 cup)
1 clove garlic, finely chopped
1/4 cup margarine or butter
4 cups 1/2-inch cubes cooked chicken
3 cups chicken broth
2 tablespoons snipped fresh cilantro (see page 7)
1 tablespoon dried basil leaves
2 teaspoons ground red chiles
1/4 teaspoon ground cloves
2 cans (16 ounces each) great northern beans
1 medium tomato, chopped (about 3/4 cup)
Blue or yellow corn tortilla chips

Cook and stir onion and garlic in margarine in 4-quart Dutch oven until onion is tender. Stir in remaining ingredients except chopped tomato and tortilla chips.

Heat to boiling; reduce heat. Cover and simmer 1 hour, stirring occasionally. Serve with tomato and tortilla chips.

6 servings (about 1½ cups each)

Butternut Squash Soup

Butternut Squash Soup

1 medium onion, chopped (about 1/2 cup)
2 tablespoons margarine or butter
2 cups chicken broth
1 pound butternut squash, pared, seeded and cut into 1-inch cubes
2 pears, pared and sliced
1 teaspoon snipped fresh thyme leaves
1/4 teaspoon salt
1/4 teaspoon white pepper
1/4 teaspoon ground coriander
1 cup whipping cream
1 unpared pear, sliced
1/2 cup chopped pecans, toasted (see To Toast, page 25)

Cook and stir onion in margarine in Dutch oven until tender. Stir in broth, squash, 2 sliced pears, thyme, salt, white pepper and coriander. Heat to boiling; reduce heat. Cover and simmer until squash is tender, 10 to 15 minutes.

Pour about half of the soup into food processor workbowl fitted with steel blade or into blender container; cover and process until smooth. Repeat with remaining soup. Return to Dutch oven; stir in whipping cream. Heat, stirring frequently, until hot. Serve with sliced pear and pecans.

6 servings (about 1 cup each)

Pasta, Rice and Other Comforts

Satisfaction is in every mouthful, cold or hot, plain or fancy. Worldwide recipes, as well as plenty from these shores, make getting your daily dose of complex carbohydrates, currently touted as a boon to dieters and fitness fanatics, a pleasure. An exotic touch like Chipotle Fettuccine with Smoked Turkey spices up a standby (page 36). You'll also find your old friend lasagne with a new look on page 38 and page 39.

Vermicelli with Lemony Green Vegetables

8 ounces uncooked vermicelli
4 cups mixed bite-size pieces green vegetables (asparagus, broccoli, Chinese pea pods, green beans, zucchini)
1/4 cup margarine or butter
1 tablespoon grated lemon peel
1/2 cup milk
1 package (3 ounces) cream cheese, cut into cubes and softened
1/2 cup grated Parmesan cheese
Salt and pepper to taste

Vermicelli with Lemony Green Vegetables

Cook vermicelli as directed on package; drain. Cook vegetables in margarine in 10-inch skillet over medium heat, stirring frequently, until crisp-tender, about 7 minutes; toss with lemon peel. Remove vegetables; keep warm.

Heat milk and cream cheese in skillet until smooth and creamy; stir in Parmesan cheese, salt and pepper. Toss with hot vermicelli. Serve vegetables over vermicelli and, if desired, with lemon wedges and coarsely ground pepper.

4 servings

CHIPOTLE FETTUCCINE WITH SMOKED TURKEY

THREE INGREDIENTS MUCH FAVORED IN SOUTHWEST COOKING (CORN, CHILES AND SMOKED MEAT) ARE INCORPORATED HERE IN A MAVERICK, CONTEMPORARY DISH.

Chipotle Fettuccine (right)
1½ cups whole kernel corn
½ cup water
1 small onion, chopped (about ¼ cup)
2 tablespoons margarine or butter
2 tablespoons all-purpose flour
½ teaspoon salt
¼ teaspoon pepper
1 cup milk
½ cup half-and-half
2 cups cut-up smoked turkey breast (about 12 ounces)

Prepare Chipotle Fettuccine. Heat corn, water and onion to boiling; reduce heat. Cover and simmer 5 minutes. Pour into food processor workbowl fitted with steel blade or into blender container; cover and process until almost smooth.

Heat margarine in 2-quart saucepan over low heat until melted. Stir in flour, salt and pepper. Cook over low heat, stirring constantly, until smooth and bubbly. Remove from heat; stir in corn mixture, milk, half-and-half and turkey. Heat to boiling, stirring constantly. Boil and stir 1 minute.

Break fettuccine into desired-size pieces. Cook fettuccine in 3 quarts boiling salted water (1 tablespoon salt) until tender, 8 to 10 minutes; drain. Toss with turkey mixture.

6 servings

CHIPOTLE FETTUCCINE

2 cups all-purpose flour
½ teaspoon salt
1 tablespoon vegetable oil
2 eggs
1 to 2 canned chipotle chiles in adobo sauce, finely chopped

Mix flour and salt in large bowl; make well in center. Beat oil, eggs and chiles; pour into well. Stir with fork, gradually bringing flour mixture to center, until dough forms a ball. If dough is too dry, mix in up to 2 tablespoons water. Roll and cut as directed below. (Use additional flour when rolling and cutting noodles.) Place fettuccine strips on towel; let stand 30 minutes.

HAND ROLLING METHOD: Knead dough on lightly floured surface until smooth and elastic, about 5 minutes. Divide into 4 equal parts. Roll dough, one part at a time, into paper-thin rectangle, about 14 x 10 inches (keep remaining dough covered). Loosely fold rectangle lengthwise into thirds; cut crosswise into ¼-inch strips. Unfold, and separate strips.

MANUAL PASTA MACHINE METHOD: Knead dough on lightly floured surface about 2 to 3 minutes. Divide dough into 4 equal parts. Feed dough, one part at a time, through smooth rollers set at widest setting (keep remaining dough covered). Sprinkle with flour if dough becomes sticky. Fold lengthwise into thirds. Repeat feeding dough through rollers and folding into thirds until dough is firm and smooth, 8 to 10 times. Feed dough through progressively narrower settings until dough is paper thin. (Dough will lengthen as it becomes thinner; it may be cut crosswise at any time for easier handling.) Feed through fettuccine cutting rollers.

Chipotle Fettuccine with Smoked Turkey

VERMICELLI WITH SMOKED FISH AND GRUYÈRE

8 ounces uncooked vermicelli
1 package (10 ounces) frozen chopped spinach
1 cup shredded Gruyère or Swiss cheese (4 ounces)
¼ cup half-and-half
2 tablespoons margarine or butter
½ pound smoked whitefish, skinned, boned and flaked into about 1-inch pieces (about 2 cups)

Cook vermicelli as directed on package except add frozen spinach to water before heating water to boiling; drain.

Toss with cheese, half-and-half and margarine. Turn onto hot platter; arrange fish on top.

4 servings

CHICKEN AND FETTUCCINE WITH DIJON SAUCE

DIJON, AN INFLUENTIAL AND ONCE-POWERFUL CITY IN THE OLD FRENCH PROVINCE OF BURGUNDY, IS FAMOUS FOR ITS MUSTARD. YOU CAN BE SURE THAT ANY DISH DESCRIBED AS "DIJON" IS FLAVORED WITH PREPARED MUSTARD.

6 ounces uncooked spinach fettuccine
½ cup chopped onion
2 cloves garlic, crushed
2 tablespoons margarine or butter
1 cup milk
½ cup chardonnay or dry white wine
2 tablespoons snipped parsley
2 tablespoons Dijon-style mustard
1 package (3 ounces) cream cheese with chives, cut into cubes
1½ cups cut-up cooked chicken or turkey

Cook fettuccine as directed on package; drain. Cook and stir onion and garlic in margarine over medium heat in 3-quart saucepan until onion is tender. Add remaining ingredients except chicken; stir until cream cheese is melted. Add chicken and hot fettuccine to cheese mixture; toss until evenly coated. Heat just until hot. Garnish with chives and freshly ground pepper if desired.

4 servings

VEGETABLE LASAGNE

3 cups chunky-style spaghetti sauce
1 medium zucchini, shredded
6 uncooked lasagne noodles
1 cup ricotta or small curd creamed cottage cheese
¼ cup grated Parmesan cheese
1 tablespoon snipped fresh oregano or 1 teaspoon dried oregano leaves
2 cups shredded mozzarella cheese (8 ounces)

Mix spaghetti sauce and zucchini. Spread 1 cup mixture in ungreased rectangular baking dish, 11 x 7 x 1½ inches; top with 3 uncooked noodles. Mix ricotta cheese, Parmesan cheese and oregano; spread over noodles in dish. Spread with 1 cup of the sauce mixture.

Top with remaining noodles, sauce mixture and the mozzarella cheese. Bake uncovered in 350° oven until hot and bubbly, about 45 minutes. Let stand 15 minutes before cutting.

8 servings

CHEESY LASAGNE

½ cup margarine or butter
½ cup all-purpose flour
½ teaspoon salt
4 cups milk
1 cup shredded Swiss cheese (4 ounces)
1 cup shredded mozzarella cheese (4 ounces)
½ cup grated Parmesan cheese
2 cups small curd creamed cottage cheese
¼ cup snipped parsley
1 tablespoon snipped fresh basil or 1 teaspoon dried basil leaves
½ teaspoon salt
1 teaspoon snipped fresh oregano or ½ teaspoon dried oregano leaves
2 cloves garlic, crushed
12 uncooked lasagne noodles
½ cup grated Parmesan cheese

Heat margarine in 2-quart saucepan over low heat until melted. Stir in flour and ½ teaspoon salt. Cook, stirring constantly, until smooth and bubbly. Remove from heat; stir in milk. Heat to boiling, stirring constantly. Boil and stir 1 minute.

Stir in Swiss cheese, mozzarella cheese and ½ cup Parmesan cheese. Cook and stir over low heat until cheeses are melted. Mix remaining ingredients except noodles and remaining Parmesan cheese.

Spread ¼ of the cheese sauce mixture in ungreased rectangular baking dish, 13 x 9 x 2 inches; top with 4 uncooked noodles. Spread 1 cup of the cottage cheese mixture over noodles; spread with ¼ of the cheese sauce mixture. Repeat with 4 noodles, the remaining cottage cheese mixture, ¼ of the cheese sauce mixture, the remaining noodles and remaining cheese sauce mixture. Sprinkle with ½ cup Parmesan cheese.

Bake uncovered in 350° oven until noodles are done, 35 to 40 minutes. Let stand 10 minutes before cutting.

12 servings

BAKED SPAGHETTI SAUCE

1 pound ground beef
1 large onion, chopped
1 clove garlic, finely chopped
1 can (10¾ ounces) condensed tomato soup
1 can (8 ounces) mushroom stems and pieces, undrained
1 can (8 ounces) tomato sauce
1 can (6 ounces) tomato paste
⅓ cup water
2 teaspoons Italian seasoning
½ teaspoon pepper
Hot cooked spaghetti
Grated Parmesan cheese

Cook and stir ground beef, onion and garlic in ovenproof Dutch oven until beef is brown; drain. Stir in remaining ingredients except spaghetti and cheese.

Cover and bake in 350° oven 1 hour; stir. Serve over spaghetti; sprinkle with cheese.

4 servings

TO MICROWAVE: Omit water and decrease Italian seasoning to 1 teaspoon. Crumble ground beef into 3-quart microwavable casserole; add onion and garlic. Cover with waxed paper and microwave on high (100%) 3 minutes; stir. Cover with waxed paper and microwave until beef is no longer pink, 2 to 3 minutes longer; drain.

Stir in remaining ingredients except spaghetti and cheese. Cover tightly and microwave 5 minutes; stir. Cover tightly and microwave on medium (50%) 15 minutes longer. Serve over spaghetti; sprinkle with cheese.

FOLLOWING PAGE: Pumpkin Ravioli with Pumpkin Seed Sauce (page 41)

PUMPKIN RAVIOLI WITH PUMPKIN SEED SAUCE

1 cup ricotta cheese
½ cup canned pumpkin
½ teaspoon salt
¼ teaspoon ground nutmeg
2 cups all-purpose flour
½ teaspoon salt
¼ cup tomato paste
1 tablespoon olive or vegetable oil
2 eggs
Pumpkin Seed Sauce (right)

Mix cheese, pumpkin, ½ teaspoon salt and the nutmeg; reserve.

Mix flour and ½ teaspoon salt in large bowl; make well in center. Beat tomato paste, oil and eggs until well blended; pour into well. Stir with fork, gradually bringing flour mixture to center, until dough forms a ball. If dough is too dry, mix in up to 2 tablespoons water. Knead on lightly floured cloth-covered surface, adding flour if dough is sticky, until smooth and elastic, about 5 minutes. Cover; let rest 5 minutes.

Divide dough into 4 equal parts. Roll dough, one part at a time, into rectangle, about 12 x 10 inches (keep remaining dough covered). Drop pumpkin mixture by 2 level teaspoonfuls onto half of the rectangle about 1½ inches apart in 2 rows of 4 mounds each. Moisten edges of dough and dough between rows of pumpkin mixture with water. Fold other half of dough up over pumpkin mixture, pressing dough down and around mixture. Trim edges with pastry wheel or knife. Cut between rows of filling to make ravioli; press edges with fork to seal. Repeat with remaining dough and pumpkin mixture. Place ravioli on towel; let stand, turning once, until dry, about 30 minutes.

Prepare Pumpkin Seed Sauce. Heat until hot; keep warm. Cook ravioli in 4 quarts boiling salted water (2 teaspoons salt) until tender, 10 to 15 minutes; drain carefully. Serve ravioli with sauce.

6 servings

PUMPKIN SEED SAUCE

1 cup shelled pumpkin seeds
1 small onion, chopped (about ¼ cup)
1 slice white bread, torn into small pieces
1 clove garlic, crushed
2 tablespoons vegetable oil
2 tablespoons canned chopped green chiles
1 can (14 ounces) chicken broth
½ cup whipping cream
Dash of salt

Cook pumpkin seeds, onion, bread and garlic in oil, stirring frequently, until bread is golden brown. Stir in chiles.

Place mixture in food processor workbowl fitted with steel blade; cover and process until smooth. Stir in broth, whipping cream and salt.

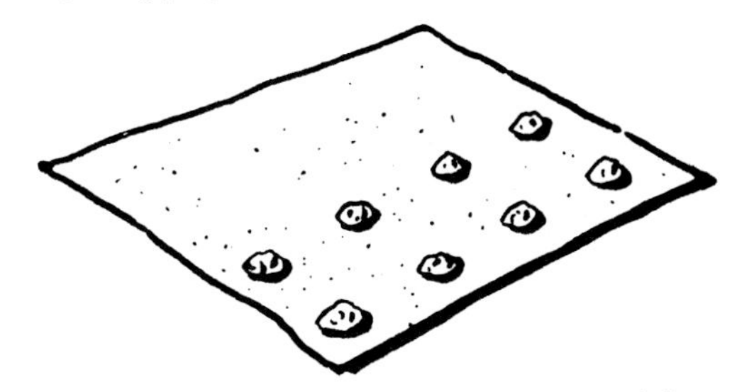

Drop pumpkin mixture by 2 level teaspoonfuls onto half of the rectangle about 1½ inches apart in 2 rows of 4 mounds each.

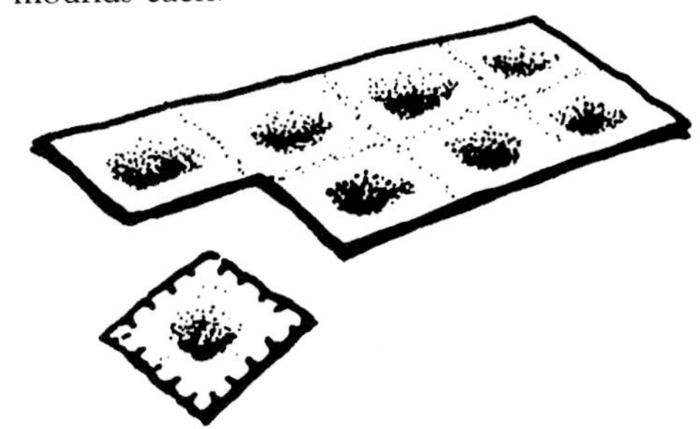

Cut between rows of filling to make ravioli; press edges with fork to seal.

PASTA WITH VEGETABLE AND GOAT CHEESE SAUCE

MILD, FRESH GOAT CHEESE, SUCH AS MONTRACHET, IS BEST FOR THIS RECIPE. GOAT CHEESE OFTEN IS REFERRED TO BY ITS FRENCH NAME, CHÈVRE.

1 tablespoon all-purpose flour
1 tablespoon instant chicken bouillon
1 teaspoon dried marjoram leaves
½ teaspoon salt
¼ teaspoon white pepper
1¼ cups water
8 ounces goat cheese, cut into ½-inch cubes
2½ cups broccoli flowerets, cut into 1¼-inch pieces
2½ cups cauliflowerets, cut into 1¼-inch pieces
¾ cup 1 x ¼ x ⅛-inch carrot strips
3 tablespoons chopped green onion
5 cups cooked spinach noodles or other pasta

Mix flour, bouillon (dry), marjoram, salt and white pepper in 2½-quart saucepan; gradually stir in water. Heat to boiling, stirring constantly. Boil and stir 1 minute; reduce heat to simmer. Stir in cheese. Cook and stir until melted, 3 to 5 minutes; keep warm.

Place steamer basket in ½ inch water in another saucepan or skillet (water should not touch bottom of basket). Place broccoli, cauliflower and carrots in basket. Cover tightly and heat to boiling; reduce heat. Steam until vegetables are crisp-tender, about 4 minutes.

Stir vegetables and onion into cheese sauce. Serve over pasta.

4 servings

VEGETABLE PIZZA WITH WHEAT GERM CRUST

Wheat Germ Crust (below)
1 cup shredded Monterey Jack cheese (4 ounces)
1 can (8 ounces) pizza sauce
1 small zucchini, thinly sliced
1 cup sliced mushrooms or 1 jar (4.5 ounces) sliced mushrooms, drained
3 green onions (with tops), sliced
1 cup shredded Cheddar cheese (4 ounces)

Heat oven to 425°. Prepare Wheat Germ Crust; sprinkle with Monterey Jack cheese. Drizzle with pizza sauce. Arrange zucchini, mushrooms and onions on pizza sauce; sprinkle with Cheddar cheese. Bake until crust is golden brown, about 20 minutes. Garnish with alfalfa sprouts and avocado slices if desired.

One 11- to 12-inch pizza

WHEAT GERM CRUST

2 cups variety baking mix
¼ cup wheat germ
⅔ cup cold water

Mix baking mix, wheat germ and water until soft dough forms; beat vigorously 20 strokes. Pat dough into 11-inch circle on greased cookie sheet, building up ½-inch edge. Or pat in greased 12-inch pizza pan with floured fingers.

RICE WITH CHAYOTE

IN ANTIGUA, WHERE THIS DISH IS OFTEN ENJOYED, CHAYOTE MIGHT BE MORE COMMONLY KNOWN AS CHRISTOPHINE. CHAYOTE IS A RELATIVE OF SQUASHES AND HAS A GENTLE FLAVOR. WITH THE ADDITION OF TOMATO, THIS IS A CLASSIC IN GUATEMALA, TOO.

2 tablespoons vegetable oil
1 medium chayote (about 8 ounces), pared and cut into ½-inch pieces
1 medium onion, chopped
2 cloves garlic, chopped
1 tablespoon vegetable oil
4 cups cooked rice
1 medium tomato, coarsely chopped
¼ teaspoon salt
Dash of pepper
Snipped chives

Heat 2 tablespoons oil in 12-inch skillet until hot. Cook and stir chayote over medium heat until crisp-tender, about 5 minutes; remove with slotted spoon.

Cook and stir onion and garlic in 1 tablespoon oil until onion is tender, about 5 minutes. Stir in rice; cook and stir until hot, about 8 minutes. Stir in chayote, tomato, salt and pepper. Cook and stir until tomato is hot, 3 to 5 minutes. Sprinkle with chives.

6 to 8 servings

PINE NUT AND GREEN ONION PILAF

A PILAF (PILAU, PILAW, PILAFF) CALLS FOR SAUTÉING THE RICE IN HOT FAT PRIOR TO COOKING IT IN BROTH. GREEN ONIONS AND LEMON PEEL GIVE THIS PILAF A LIVELY FLAVOR THAT WOULD BE SUPERB WITH ANY SAUCY FISH.

1 cup uncooked regular rice
½ cup sliced green onions (with tops)
½ cup pine nuts (2 ounces)
2 tablespoons margarine or butter
2½ cups chicken broth
1 teaspoon grated lemon peel
¼ teaspoon salt
¼ cup sliced green onion tops

Cook and stir rice, ½ cup onions and the pine nuts in margarine in 3-quart saucepan until nuts are light brown, about 5 minutes. Stir in remaining ingredients except ¼ cup onion tops.

Heat to boiling, stirring once or twice; reduce heat. Cover and simmer 14 minutes. (Do not lift cover or stir.) Remove from heat; fluff rice lightly with fork. Cover and let steam 5 to 10 minutes. Sprinkle with onion tops.

6 servings

Lemon and Celery Pilaf

This Portuguese pilaf adds the zip of mustard and red pepper sauce to lemon's fresh effect. The result is a fluffy dish that is great with broiled or baked fish.

1 small onion, chopped
1 small clove garlic, finely chopped
¼ cup margarine or butter
2 cups water
1 cup uncooked regular rice
2 stalks celery, sliced
2 teaspoons instant chicken bouillon
2 teaspoons finely shredded lemon peel
½ teaspoon salt
¼ teaspoon dry mustard
⅛ teaspoon red pepper sauce
2 tablespoons snipped parsley

Cook and stir onion and garlic in margarine in 3-quart saucepan until onion is tender. Stir in remaining ingredients except parsley. Heat to boiling, stirring once or twice; reduce heat. Cover and simmer 14 minutes. (Do not lift cover or stir.) Remove from heat. Stir in parsley lightly with fork; cover and let steam 5 to 10 minutes.

7 servings

Indonesian Yellow Rice

Coconut milk, lemon grass and turmeric are the key elements that flavor this fluffy rice.

2 cups Coconut Milk (below)
1 cup uncooked regular rice
1 piece lemon grass (see page 7), about 2 inches long
½ teaspoon salt
¼ teaspoon ground turmeric

Heat all ingredients to boiling in 2-quart saucepan, stirring once or twice; reduce heat. Cover and simmer 14 minutes. (Do not lift cover or stir.) Remove from heat. Fluff rice lightly with fork; cover and let steam 5 to 10 minutes. Remove lemon grass.

6 servings

Coconut Milk

1 cup chopped fresh coconut (see Note)
1 cup hot water

Place coconut and hot water in blender container. Cover and blend on high speed until coconut is finely chopped. Strain through several layers of cheesecloth. Cover and refrigerate no longer than 48 hours.

Note: To open coconut, puncture eyes of coconut with ice pick; drain liquid. Bake coconut in 375° oven 12 to 15 minutes. Remove from oven. Tap shell with hammer to open. Cut meat out of shell. Pare brown skin from coconut meat.

Extra rich coconut cream will rise to the top after a few hours tightly covered in the refrigerator. Skim off and use, or stir back into milk.

POLENTA WITH CHEESE

THE RUMANIANS HAVE THEIR OWN VERSION OF THIS ITALIAN CLASSIC: MAMALIGA. FRIED, POLENTA CAN BE ENJOYED AS EITHER A SWEET OR SAVORY TREAT.

1 cup yellow cornmeal
¾ cup water
3¼ cups boiling water
2 teaspoons salt
1 tablespoon margarine or butter
1 cup grated Parmesan cheese
⅓ cup shredded Swiss or Kashkaval cheese (about 1½ ounces)

Mix cornmeal and ¾ cup water in 2-quart saucepan. Stir in 3¼ cups water and the salt. Cook, stirring constantly, until mixture thickens and boils; reduce heat. Cover and simmer, stirring occasionally, 10 minutes. Remove from heat; stir until smooth.

Spread ⅓ of the mixture in greased 1½-quart casserole. Dot with ⅓ of the margarine; sprinkle with ⅓ of the Parmesan cheese. Repeat twice. Sprinkle with Swiss cheese. Cook uncovered in 350° oven until hot and bubbly, 15 to 20 minutes.

6 servings

FRIED CORNMEAL MUSH: Omit margarine and the grated Parmesan and Swiss cheeses. After cooking 10 minutes, spread in greased loaf pan, 9 x 5 x 3 inches. Cover and refrigerate until firm, at least 12 hours. Invert pan to unmold; cut into ½-inch slices.

Heat 2 tablespoons margarine in 10-inch skillet until melted. Coat slices with flour; cook uncovered in margarine over low heat until brown, about 5 minutes on each side. Serve with molasses, jam, maple syrup or sour cream if desired.

SERRANO GRITS WITH CHEESE

A RIB-STICKING SIDE DISH, THIS VERSION, FEATURING FIERY SERRANOS, DELICIOUSLY HOLDS ITS OWN WITH STEAK OR VENISON.

½ cup chopped red bell pepper
½ cup sliced green onions (with tops)
2 serrano chiles, seeded and chopped
2 tablespoons margarine or butter
1½ cups milk
1½ cups water
½ teaspoon salt
¼ teaspoon pepper
¾ cup white hominy quick grits
1½ cups shredded Monterey Jack cheese (6 ounces)

Cook and stir bell pepper, onions and chiles in margarine in 10-inch skillet until pepper is tender.

Heat milk, water, salt and pepper to boiling in 2-quart saucepan. Gradually add grits, stirring constantly; reduce heat. Simmer uncovered, stirring frequently, until thick about 5 minutes. Stir in bell pepper mixture and cheese.

6 servings

OF CABBAGES AND CACTUS

The age-old admonition, "Eat your vegetables," is more promise than threat these days. Vegetables have become not only side dish health heroes, but the focus of the main course, too. No longer just boiled and buttered, vegetables are stir-fried, steamed, tossed and braised as well as tossed fresh into original salads. And what vegetables! Jicama, cactus and chayote have joined the ranks of peas, beans and tomatoes. See page 6 for an introduction to some new-to-the-U.S. produce.

RADISH AND WATERCRESS SALAD

THE EUROPEANS TEND TO EAT WATERCRESS MORE THAN WE DO. ITS PEPPERY FLAVOR IS A NICE COMPLEMENT TO THE RADISHES.

8 ounces watercress
3 tablespoons olive or vegetable oil
1 tablespoon white wine vinegar
1/4 teaspoon salt
Freshly ground pepper
12 radishes, sliced

Remove tough stems from watercress; break sprigs into bite-size pieces. Arrange watercress on plates. Mix oil, vinegar, salt and pepper. Pour over radishes; toss. Spoon radish mixture over watercress.

6 servings

Clockwise from left: French Garden Peas, French Potato Salad (page 48) and Radish and Watercress Salad

FRENCH GARDEN PEAS

IN FRANCE, THE ARRIVAL OF THE FIRST SWEET PEAS (PETITS POIS) IS CAUSE FOR CELEBRATION.

1 1/2 cups shelled fresh green peas (1 1/2 pounds in pods)*
1 cup shredded lettuce
3 green onions, sliced
2 tablespoons water
2 tablespoons margarine or butter
1/2 teaspoon salt
1/4 teaspoon sugar
Dash of pepper

Heat all ingredients to boiling; reduce heat. Cover and simmer until peas are tender, about 8 minutes.

4 servings

**1 package (10 ounces) frozen green peas can be substituted for the fresh peas.*

FRENCH POTATO SALAD

THE FRENCH LIKE TO FLAVOR THEIR POTATOES WITH WINE, NATURELLEMENT. THE DRESSING INCLUDES TARRAGON AND DARK MUSTARD, BOTH TRADITIONAL ELEMENTS OF AN HERBAL VINAIGRETTE.

6 medium potatoes (about 2 pounds)
1 clove garlic, cut into halves
¼ teaspoon instant beef or chicken bouillon
⅓ cup hot water
⅓ cup dry white wine
Tarragon Dressing (below)
3 tablespoons snipped parsley

Heat 1 inch salted water (½ teaspoon salt to 1 cup water) to boiling. Add potatoes. Heat to boiling; reduce heat. Cover and cook until tender, 30 to 35 minutes. Drain and cool.

Rub 2-quart bowl with garlic; discard garlic. Cut potatoes into ¼-inch slices; place in bowl. Dissolve bouillon in hot water; add wine. Pour over potatoes. Cover and refrigerate, stirring once or twice; drain.

Prepare Tarragon Dressing; gently toss with potatoes. Sprinkle with parsley. Garnish with tomato wedges and sliced cooked luncheon meat if desired.

4 to 6 servings

TARRAGON DRESSING

3 tablespoons olive or vegetable oil
2 tablespoons tarragon vinegar
2 teaspoons snipped chives
1 teaspoon salt
1 teaspoon dark prepared mustard
½ teaspoon dried tarragon leaves
⅛ teaspoon pepper

Shake all ingredients in tightly covered jar.

FRESH HERB AND TOMATO SALAD

CHOOSE THE REDDEST, RIPEST TOMATOES YOU CAN FIND FOR THIS VARIATION OF AN IRANIAN DISH, A CELEBRATION OF SUMMER'S MOST TEMPTING HERBS.

3 large tomatoes, sliced
⅓ cup flat-leaf parsley or curly parsley leaves
¼ cup fresh cilantro leaves (see page 7)
¼ cup fresh mint leaves
2 tablespoons fresh tarragon leaves
2 green onions (with tops), thinly sliced
¼ cup crumbled feta cheese
Plain yogurt

Arrange tomatoes on serving platter. Mix remaining ingredients except cheese and yogurt; sprinkle over tomatoes. Sprinkle cheese over herbs. Serve with yogurt.

6 servings

TOMATOES, PEPPERS AND ONIONS

THIS IS A ROMAN FAVORITE, HOT OR COLD. TOSS MARINATED OLIVES INTO THIS DISH IF YOU LIKE.

2 medium onions, sliced
2 tablespoons olive or vegetable oil
3 medium green peppers, cut into strips
1 teaspoon dried basil leaves
1 teaspoon red wine vinegar
½ teaspoon salt
¼ teaspoon pepper
2 medium tomatoes, coarsely chopped (about 2 cups)

Cook and stir onions in oil in 10-inch skillet until tender; add remaining ingredients except tomatoes. Cover and cook over low heat 10 minutes. Add tomatoes. Cover and simmer until green pepper is tender, about 5 minutes. Garnish with ripe olives if desired.

4 servings

ITALIAN TOMATO AND BREAD SALAD

THIS RECIPE, AT ITS BEST WITH BURSTING RIPE TOMATOES, IS FAR MORE THAN A SUMMERY USE FOR STALE BREAD. PUNGENT BASIL AND RED TOMATOES ARE THE FEATURED COMBINATION, WITH GOOD OLIVE OIL AND RED WINE VINEGAR SOAKING INTO THE BREAD CHUNKS.

4 cups 1-inch pieces stale Italian or French bread
2 medium tomatoes, cut into bite-size pieces
2 cloves garlic, finely chopped
1 medium green pepper, cut into bite-size pieces
⅓ cup snipped fresh basil leaves
2 tablespoons snipped parsley
⅓ cup olive oil
2 tablespoons red wine vinegar
½ teaspoon salt
⅛ teaspoon pepper

Mix bread, tomatoes, garlic, green pepper, basil and parsley. Shake remaining ingredients in tightly covered container. Pour over bread mixture; toss. Cover and refrigerate at least 1 hour. Garnish with Kalamata or Greek olives if desired.

6 servings (about 1 cup each)

CAESAR BEAN SALAD

YOU CAN KEEP MOST OF THESE INGREDIENTS ON HAND IN YOUR PANTRY TO WHIP TOGETHER ANYTIME.

1 can (16 ounces) great northern beans, drained
1 can (15½ ounces) red kidney beans, drained
1 can (15 ounces) garbanzo beans, drained
½ cup sweet pickle relish
½ cup Caesar dressing
¼ cup snipped parsley
Salt and pepper to taste
Lemon wedges

Mix all ingredients except salt, pepper and lemon wedges in large bowl. Cover and refrigerate at least 1 hour, stirring occasionally.

Remove with slotted spoon and, if desired, arrange on salad greens; sprinkle with salt and pepper and, if desired, additional snipped parsley and grated Parmesan cheese. Garnish with lemon wedges.

5 servings

CAESAR BEAN SALAD WITH AVOCADOS: For each salad, place avocado half on salad plate. Spoon about ½ cup bean mixture onto avocado.

CAESAR BEAN SALAD WITH TOMATOES: For each salad, arrange 2 large slices tomato on salad plate. Spoon about ½ cup bean mixture onto tomato slices.

Rio Grande Melon Salad

2 cups watermelon balls
2 mangoes or papayas (see page 7), pared and sliced
½ honeydew melon, pared, seeded and thinly sliced
¾ cup seedless red grape halves
1 large bunch watercress
Honey-Lime Dressing (below)

Arrange fruits on watercress. Drizzle with Honey-Lime Dressing.

6 servings

Honey-Lime Dressing

⅓ cup vegetable oil
¼ teaspoon grated lime peel
2 tablespoons lime juice
1 tablespoon honey

Shake all ingredients in tightly covered container.

Texas Slaw with Cumin Dressing

Cumin Dressing (right)
1 small head green cabbage, finely shredded (about 3 cups)
1 small head red cabbage, finely shredded (about 3 cups)
1 small red bell pepper, thinly sliced
1 small yellow bell pepper, thinly sliced
1 to 2 jalapeño chiles, seeded and finely chopped
2 tablespoons snipped fresh cilantro (see page 7)

Prepare Cumin Dressing. Mix remaining ingredients. Just before serving, toss with Cumin Dressing.

10 to 12 servings

Cumin Dressing

½ cup sour cream
½ cup plain yogurt
2 teaspoons sugar
½ teaspoon salt
½ teaspoon ground cumin
¼ teaspoon pepper

Mix all ingredients. Cover and refrigerate 1 hour.

Jicama Citrus Salad with Sangria Dressing

Jicama has a crisp texture almost like water chestnuts. Under the brown skin is snowy, crunchy flesh.

3 large oranges, pared and sectioned
2 red grapefruit, pared and sectioned
1 medium jicama (see page 7) (about 1 pound), pared and cut into ½-inch cubes
Sangria Dressing (below)

Arrange oranges, grapefruit and jicama on 8 salad plates or mix together. Serve with Sangria Dressing.

8 servings

Sangria Dressing

¼ cup vegetable oil
¼ cup dry red wine
2 tablespoons honey
2 tablespoons orange juice

Shake all ingredients in tightly covered container.

Rio Grande Melon Salad

CRACKED WHEAT AND PARSLEY SALAD

DRAIN THE SOFTENED BULGUR THOROUGHLY, SO THAT THE GRAINS WILL ABSORB ALL THE GOOD FLAVOR OF THE LEMONY DRESSING. EVEN SUCH A SMALL QUANTITY OF FRESH MINT AS 2 TABLESPOONS MAKES AN EXCITING CHANGE FROM WESTERN-STYLE SEASONING. THIS BULGUR SALAD FROM THE MIDDLE EAST WOULD BENEFIT FROM A SCATTERING OF MARINATED OLIVES.

¾ cup bulgur (cracked wheat)
1½ cups snipped parsley
3 medium tomatoes, chopped
⅓ cup chopped green onions (with tops)
2 tablespoons snipped fresh mint or 2 teaspoons crushed dried mint leaves
¼ cup olive or vegetable oil
¼ cup lemon juice
1 teaspoon salt
¼ teaspoon pepper

Cover bulgur with cold water; let stand 30 minutes. Drain; press out as much water as possible. Place bulgur, parsley, tomatoes, green onions and mint in glass or plastic bowl. Mix remaining ingredients; pour over bulgur mixture. Toss. Cover and refrigerate at least 1 hour. Garnish with ripe olives if desired.

6 servings

Note: For a softer texture, cover bulgur with boiling water; let stand 1 hour.

Fresh Herb and Tomato Salad (page 48) and Cracked Wheat and Parsley Salad

HEARTS OF PALM IN TOMATO SAUCE

THE CABBAGE PALMETTO TREE, WHEN YOUNG, YIELDS AT THE CENTER OF ITS STEM A FIBROUS MEAT THAT IS NEARLY WHITE AND ABSOLUTELY DELICIOUS. CANNED HEARTS OF PALM HAVE BEEN BOILED. IN THE DOMINICAN REPUBLIC, THIS EXOTIC VEGETABLE IS STEWED IN A TOMATO SAUCE WITH HAM AND JALAPEÑO PEPPERS.

1 medium onion, chopped
2 cloves garlic, finely chopped
1 jalapeño chile, seeded and chopped
4 ounces fully cooked smoked ham, coarsely chopped (about ⅔ cup)
2 tablespoons vegetable oil
1 can (16 ounces) whole tomatoes (with liquid)
2 tablespoons snipped parsley
1 teaspoon vinegar
⅛ teaspoon pepper
2 cans (14 ounces each) hearts of palm, rinsed, drained and sliced ½ inch thick
Grated Parmesan cheese

Cook and stir onion, garlic, jalapeño chile and ham in oil in 10-inch skillet over medium heat until onion is tender. Add tomatoes, parsley, vinegar and pepper; break up tomatoes with fork. Heat to boiling; reduce heat. Simmer uncovered, stirring occasionally, until mixture is thickened, about 15 minutes. Stir in hearts of palm. Cover and simmer, stirring occasionally, until hearts of palm are hot, about 5 minutes. Sprinkle with cheese.

6 servings

INDONESIAN SALAD WITH COCONUT-PEANUT DRESSING

INDONESIA WAS HISTORICALLY A STOPPING POINT FOR EXPLORERS AND TRADE SHIPS, AND HER CUISINE REFLECTS THE INFLUENCE OF OTHER CULTURES. THIS CRUNCHY-SWEET CONFETTI SALAD HAS A STRONG PEANUT FLAVOR.

Coconut-Peanut Dressing (right)
1 cup bean sprouts
1 cup shredded cabbage
4 ounces bean curd (tofu) drained and cut into 1-inch pieces
2 tablespoons peanut or vegetable oil
1 cup sliced cooked potatoes
1 cup cooked cut green beans
1 cup cooked sliced carrots
1 medium cucumber, sliced
2 hard-cooked eggs, peeled and sliced

Prepare Coconut-Peanut Dressing. Pour enough boiling water over bean sprouts and cabbage to cover; let stand 2 minutes. Drain.

Cook bean curd in oil in 10-inch skillet over medium heat, turning pieces gently, until light brown. Remove with slotted spoon; drain. Cook potatoes in same skillet until light brown; drain.

Arrange bean sprouts, cabbage, bean curd, potatoes and remaining ingredients on platter. Pour dressing over salad.

6 to 8 servings

COCONUT-PEANUT DRESSING

½ cup flaked coconut
1 cup hot water
1 small onion, chopped
1 clove garlic, finely chopped
1½ teaspoons peanut oil or Ghee (see page 60)
⅔ cup peanut butter
½ cup water
1 tablespoon sugar
½ teaspoon salt
¼ to ½ teaspoon chili powder
⅛ teaspoon ground ginger

Place coconut in blender container; add 1 cup water. Cover and blend on high speed about 30 seconds.

Cook and stir onion and garlic in oil in 2-quart saucepan until onion is tender, about 5 minutes. Stir in coconut and remaining ingredients. Heat to boiling, stirring constantly; reduce heat. Simmer uncovered, stirring occasionally, until slightly thickened, about 3 minutes. Serve warm.

Indonesian Salad with Coconut-Peanut Dressing

Grilled Corn with Chile-Lime Spread

FRESH CORN GRILLED IN ITS HUSK HAS A MATCHLESS FLAVOR, ESPECIALLY WHEN THE CORN IS SLATHERED WITH CHILE-LIME SPREAD BEFORE COOKING.

½ cup margarine or butter, softened
½ teaspoon grated lime peel
3 tablespoons lime juice
1 to 2 teaspoons ground red chiles
6 ears corn (with husks)

Mix all ingredients except corn. Remove large outer husks from each ear corn; turn back inner husks, and remove silk. Spread each ear corn with about 2 teaspoons margarine mixture; reserve remaining margarine mixture.

Pull husks up over ears; tie with fine wire to secure. Grill corn 3 inches from medium coals, turning frequently, until done, 20 to 30 minutes. Serve with remaining margarine mixture.

6 servings

ROAST CORN WITH CHILE-LIME SPREAD: Heat oven to 475°. Prepare corn as directed. Roast in ungreased jelly roll pan, 15½ x 10½ x 1 inch, turning frequently, until done, 30 to 35 minutes.

Grilled Corn with Chile-Lime Spread

Baked Chayotes with Tomatoes

ALSO KNOWN AS MIRLITONS OR VEGETABLE PEARS, CHAYOTES GROW ON SQUASHLIKE VINES IN THE SOUTHERN UNITED STATES. THEY ARE GREEN AND PEAR-SHAPED, AVERAGING ABOUT 6 TO 7 INCHES IN LENGTH.

4 medium chayotes
2 slices bacon, cut into ½-inch pieces
2 tablespoons vegetable oil
½ teaspoon salt
½ teaspoon dried oregano leaves
¼ teaspoon ground nutmeg
¼ teaspoon pepper
4 medium tomatoes, chopped (about 4 cups)
1 large onion, chopped (about 1 cup)
1 clove garlic, finely chopped
1 cup shredded Monterey Jack cheese (4 ounces)

Pare chayotes; cut lengthwise into fourths. Remove seeds. Heat enough salted water to cover chayotes (½ teaspoon salt to 1 cup water) to boiling. Add chayotes. Cover and boil until crisp-tender, 15 to 20 minutes; drain. Arrange chayotes in ungreased rectangular baking dish, 13 x 9 x 2 inches.

Cook and stir bacon in 2-quart saucepan until crisp. Stir in remaining ingredients except cheese. Heat to boiling; reduce heat. Simmer uncovered 15 minutes.

Heat oven to 350°. Pour vegetable mixture over chayotes; sprinkle with cheese. Bake uncovered until hot and bubbly and cheese is melted, about 15 minutes.

8 servings

CINNAMON SQUASH RINGS

2 tablespoons packed brown sugar
2 tablespoons milk
1 egg
¾ cup soft bread crumbs (about 2½ slices bread)
¼ cup yellow or white cornmeal
2 teaspoons ground cinnamon
1 large acorn squash (about 1½ pounds), cut crosswise into ½-inch slices and seeded
⅓ cup margarine or butter, melted

Heat oven to 400°. Mix brown sugar, milk and egg. Mix bread crumbs, cornmeal and cinnamon. Dip squash slices into egg mixture, and coat with bread crumb mixture; repeat.

Place in ungreased rectangular pan, 13 x 9 x 2 inches; drizzle with margarine. Bake uncovered until squash is tender, 30 to 35 minutes.

6 servings

CAULIFLOWER WITH SPICES

THIS INDIAN DISH IS GILDED WITH THE CHARACTERISTIC BRIGHT YELLOW OF TURMERIC. IF BLACK MUSTARD SEED IS UNAVAILABLE, YELLOW MUSTARD SEED MAY BE SUBSTITUTED.

¼ cup vegetable oil
2 teaspoons black mustard seed
1 teaspoon fennel seed
2 cloves garlic, finely chopped
¼ teaspoon ground turmeric
⅛ teaspoon ground red pepper
1 small head cauliflower (about 2½ pounds) separated into flowerets
¼ cup water
½ teaspoon salt

Heat oil in 12-inch skillet until hot. Cook and stir mustard and fennel seeds over medium heat until mustard seed pops, about 2 minutes. Add garlic, turmeric and red pepper. Cook and stir until garlic is light brown.

Stir in remaining ingredients. Heat to boiling; reduce heat. Simmer uncovered, stirring occasionally, until cauliflower is crisp-tender and liquid is evaporated, 18 to 20 minutes.

6 servings

BAKED PLANTAINS

LATIN KITCHENS FREQUENTLY COOK THE PLANTAIN AS A STARCHY VEGETABLE. IT HAS MUCH THE SAME FLAVOR, THOUGH NOT THE SAME SWEETNESS, AS A BANANA. HERE THE PLANTAIN IS BAKED MUCH LIKE A POTATO.

4 ripe plantains
Vegetable oil
Margarine or butter, melted
Salt

Cut tip off each end of plantains. Cut lengthwise slit through peel on one side of each plantain. Rub peel of plantains with oil.

Arrange plantains, cut sides up, in ungreased rectangular baking dish, 13 x 9 x 2 inches. Cook uncovered in 350° oven until tender when pierced with fork, about 35 minutes. Make 1 or 2 lengthwise cuts through peel; remove peel. Serve plantains with margarine and salt.

8 servings

Cinnamon Squash Rings

SAVORY GREEN BEANS WITH COCONUT

DON'T EXPECT THESE BEANS TO BE BARELY COOKED AND CRISP. THEY ARE GENTLY STEWED IN CLARIFIED BUTTER WITH COCONUT AND AROMATIC INDIAN SPICES. THIS WOULD BE DELICIOUS WITH CURRIES OR A SIMPLE PORK ROAST.

¼ cup Ghee (below)
½ cup flaked coconut
½ cup water
1½ pounds green beans
1 medium onion, sliced
1 teaspoon ground coriander
½ teaspoon ground turmeric
½ teaspoon ground ginger
1½ teaspoons salt

Prepare Ghee. Place coconut and water in blender container. Cover and blend on high speed until coconut is finely chopped, about 10 seconds. Cut beans lengthwise into halves; cut halves lengthwise into halves.

Cook and stir onion, coriander, turmeric and ginger in Ghee in 10-inch skillet over medium heat until onion is coated. Stir coconut mixture, beans and salt into onion mixture. Cover and cook over medium heat, stirring occasionally, until beans are tender, 20 to 30 minutes.

4 to 5 servings

GHEE

1 pound unsalted butter

Cut butter into pieces. Heat over low heat until melted. Increase heat to medium; heat to boiling. Immediately remove from heat and stir gently. Return to heat; slowly heat to simmering. Simmer uncovered until butter separates into transparent substance on top and milk solids on bottom, 30 to 40 minutes. Remove from heat; let stand 5 minutes. Strain through cheesecloth into container. Cover and refrigerate no longer than 2 months.

SPICY CABBAGE

THIS SEPHARDIC DISH IS SPICED WITH ELEMENTS THAT TELL OF ITS INDIAN AND MIDDLE EASTERN ORIGINS: JALAPEÑO PEPPERS, CUMIN, CORIANDER AND TURMERIC.

2 tablespoons vegetable oil
1 medium onion, chopped
2 cloves garlic, finely chopped
2 jalapeño chiles, seeded and chopped
1 medium green or red pepper, chopped
½ teaspoon ground cumin
½ teaspoon ground coriander
½ teaspoon ground turmeric
½ teaspoon salt
2 medium tomatoes, coarsely chopped
1 small head green cabbage (about 1½ pounds), thinly sliced
1 tablespoon vinegar

Heat oil in 12-inch skillet until hot. Cook and stir onion, garlic, jalapeño chiles, green pepper, cumin, coriander, turmeric and salt over medium heat until onion is tender, about 5 minutes. Stir in tomatoes and cabbage. Heat to boiling; reduce heat. Cover and simmer until cabbage is tender, about 12 minutes. Stir in vinegar.

8 servings

SUGAR-BROWNED POTATOES

DENMARK'S SWEET TOOTH FAVORS THESE LITTLE GOLDEN BROWN POTATOES.

2 pounds new potatoes
¼ cup margarine or butter
¼ cup sugar
½ teaspoon salt
3 tablespoons water

Heat 1 inch salted water (1 teaspoon salt to 1 cup water) to boiling. Add potatoes. Heat to boiling; reduce heat. Cover and cook until tender, 20 to 25 minutes; drain.

Cook and stir margarine, sugar and salt in 10-inch skillet over medium heat until mixture starts to turn golden brown. Remove from heat; cool slightly. Stir in water until blended. Add potatoes. Cook over low heat, turning potatoes to coat with sugar mixture.

4 to 6 servings

MASHED POTATOES WITH CABBAGE

FOR THIS IRISH DISH, TENDER, COOKED CABBAGE IS STIRRED INTO CREAMY MASHED POTATOES—SIMPLE AND DELICIOUS.

6 medium potatoes (about 2 pounds)
½ head green cabbage, shredded (about 3 cups)
6 green onions (with tops), chopped
¼ cup water
⅛ teaspoon salt
⅓ to ½ cup milk
¼ cup margarine or butter, softened
1 teaspoon salt
Dash of pepper
Margarine or butter

Heat 1 inch salted water (½ teaspoon salt to 1 cup water) to boiling. Add potatoes. Heat to boiling; reduce heat. Cover and cook until tender, 30 to 35 minutes; drain. Heat cabbage, onions, water and ⅛ teaspoon salt to boiling; reduce heat. Cover and simmer until crisp-tender, 5 to 10 minutes; drain.

Mash potatoes until no lumps remain. Beat in milk in small amounts. Add ¼ cup margarine, 1 teaspoon salt and the pepper; beat until potatoes are light and fluffy. Stir in cabbage and onions; dot with margarine.

6 servings

RED ONION-TOPPED POTATOES

THESE SAVORY POTATOES WOULD BE DELICIOUS WITH ANY GRILLED MAIN DISH. FRESH, ACID CILANTRO SPARKS THE RICH TOPPING OF CHEESE AND ONIONS.

3 large baking potatoes (about 1½ pounds)
Salt and pepper to taste
1 cup grated queso añejo or Romano cheese
¾ cup finely chopped red onion
1 tablespoon snipped fresh cilantro (see page 7)
1 clove garlic, finely chopped

Heat oven to 375°. Bake potatoes until tender, about 1 hour.

Cut potatoes lengthwise into halves; score top of potatoes crisscross fashion, being careful not to cut through skin. Sprinkle with salt and pepper.

Mix remaining ingredients. Divide mixture among potatoes. Press into scores and on top of each potato. Bake until hot, about 5 minutes.

6 servings

Caramelized Sweet Potatoes

A most untraditional treatment for an old favorite combines sweet potatoes with Jerusalem artichokes, also known as "sunchokes," a relative of the sunflower.

1½ pounds sweet potatoes, pared and coarsely shredded
½ pound Jerusalem artichokes, pared and coarsely shredded
½ cup margarine or butter, melted
¼ cup sugar

Mix potatoes, artichokes and margarine; reserve. Heat sugar in 10-inch skillet over medium heat until melted and light brown, about 10 minutes.

Stir in potato mixture; cook, stirring occasionally, until potatoes are tender, about 15 minutes.

8 servings

Southwest Vegetable Sauté

Lime Butter Sauce (right)
1 medium onion, finely chopped (about ½ cup)
2 cloves garlic, finely chopped
¼ cup margarine or butter
4 very small pattypan squash (about 4 ounces each), cut into halves
2 small zucchini, cut into ¼-inch strips
2 small yellow squash, cut into ¼-inch strips
1 medium chayote, pared, seeded and cut into ½-inch cubes
1 small red bell pepper, cut into thin rings
1 small yellow bell pepper, cut into thin rings
½ teaspoon salt
¼ teaspoon ground red pepper
8 fresh squash blossoms, if desired

Prepare Lime Butter Sauce; reserve. Cook and stir onion and garlic in margarine in Dutch oven until onion is tender.

Stir in remaining ingredients except squash blossoms. Cook over medium heat, stirring occasionally, until vegetables are crisp-tender; stir in squash blossoms. Serve with Lime Butter Sauce.

8 servings

Lime Butter Sauce

Make this lime hollandaise with butter only. It is delicious on seafood and cooked vegetables and as a sauce for egg dishes in the tradition of Eggs Benedict.

2 egg yolks
1 tablespoon lime juice
*½ cup firm butter**
½ teaspoon grated lime peel

Stir egg yolks and lime juice vigorously in 1½-quart saucepan. Add ¼ cup of the butter. Heat over very low heat, stirring constantly, until butter is melted.

Add remaining butter. Continue heating, stirring vigorously, until butter is melted and sauce is thickened. (Be sure butter melts slowly so that sauce will thicken without curdling.) Stir in lime peel. Serve hot or at room temperature. Cover and refrigerate any remaining sauce.

Margarine is not recommended.

Southwest Vegetable Sauté

The Main Course, of Course

Suppers used to focus exclusively on chicken, beef or pork. But nowadays, duck, pheasant and Cornish hens, even buffalo burgers and rabbit are easy enough for any cook, tasty enough for any company. New ways with the old standbys take inspiration from the world over, and a number of main dishes boast no meat at all.

Chicken with Red Peppers

FRESH RED PEPPERS AND PROSCIUTTO FLAVOR THIS LIGHTLY FRIED CHICKEN. IN SPAIN BOTH RIPE AND GREEN OLIVES ARE SERVED AS AN ACCOMPANIMENT.

2 tablespoons vegetable oil
3- to 3½-pound broiler-fryer chicken, cut up
1 medium onion, chopped
1 clove garlic, chopped
3 medium red peppers, cut into thin strips
2 medium tomatoes, chopped
½ cup chopped prosciutto (about 2 ounces)
1 teaspoon salt
¼ teaspoon pepper

Chicken with Red Peppers

Heat oil in 12-inch skillet until hot. Cook chicken over medium heat until brown on all sides, about 15 minutes; remove chicken. Cook and stir onion and garlic in oil until onion is tender. Stir in remaining ingredients. Heat to boiling; reduce heat.

Return chicken to skillet. Simmer uncovered, turning chicken pieces occasionally, until thickest pieces of chicken are done, about 40 minutes. Remove chicken to warm platter; keep warm. Cook and stir sauce over medium heat until very thick, about 5 minutes; serve over chicken. Garnish with ripe or Kalamata olives if desired.

6 servings

CHICKEN WITH FIGS IN PORT SAUCE

2 large whole chicken breasts (about 2 pounds)
2 tablespoons margarine or butter
1 cup tawny port or sweet red wine
½ cup whipping cream
¼ cup sliced green onions (with tops)
1 tablespoon finely shredded orange peel
6 sun-dried figs, cut into fourths
6 slices bacon, crisply cooked and crumbled
Hot cooked rice

Remove skin and bones from chicken breasts; cut each whole chicken breast into halves. Flatten each half breast to ½-inch thickness between plastic wrap or waxed paper, being careful not to tear chicken.

Heat margarine in 10-inch skillet over medium heat until melted. Cook chicken in margarine, turning once, until light brown, 15 to 20 minutes. Add port. Heat to boiling; reduce heat. Cover and simmer until chicken is done, 15 to 20 minutes. Remove chicken to warm platter; keep warm.

Add whipping cream to skillet. Heat to boiling; cook uncovered until very thick, about 8 minutes. Stir in remaining ingredients except rice. Cook, stirring occasionally, until figs are hot, about 3 minutes. Place chicken pieces on rice; spoon sauce over chicken and rice. Garnish with orange sections and sprigs of fresh herb if desired.

4 servings

MOROCCAN CHICKEN WITH OLIVES

LEMON SHARPENS THE SPICY SAUCE OF THIS TAGINE, A MOROCCAN SPECIALTY. TRADITIONALLY KALAMATA OLIVES (LIGHT-COLORED BLACK OLIVES) GARNISH THIS DISH TO ADD A SLIGHTLY SALTY FLAVOR. PRESERVED LEMONS ARE AN AUTHENTIC INGREDIENT, ADDING AN ADDITIONAL SALTY-SOUR FLAVOR; USING FRESH LEMON INSTEAD HOLDS THE KITCHEN TIME TO A MINIMUM.

¼ cup snipped fresh cilantro (see page 7)
1 tablespoon paprika
2 teaspoons ground cumin
½ teaspoon salt
½ teaspoon ground turmeric
½ teaspoon ground ginger
2 cloves garlic, finely chopped
3- to 3½-pound broiler-fryer chicken, cut up
⅓ cup all-purpose flour
½ cup water
¼ cup lemon juice
1 teaspoon instant chicken bouillon
½ cup Kalamata or Greek olives
1 lemon, sliced

Mix cilantro, paprika, cumin, salt, turmeric, ginger and garlic. Rub mixture on all sides of chicken; coat with flour. Place chicken in ungreased rectangular baking dish, 13 x 9 x 2 inches. Mix water, lemon juice and bouillon; pour over chicken. Add olives and lemon slices. Cook uncovered in 350° oven, spooning juices over chicken occasionally, until thickest pieces of chicken are done, about 1 hour. Serve with couscous or rice if desired.

6 servings

GRILLED LEMON CHICKEN

COMBINING MICROWAVE AND GRILL RESULTS IN FLAWLESS, FLAVORFUL CHICKEN THAT IS THOROUGHLY COOKED WITHOUT BEING SCORCHED BY THE FLAMES.

2½- to 3-pound broiler-fryer chicken, cut up
½ cup dry white wine
¼ cup lemon juice
2 tablespoons vegetable oil
1 teaspoon paprika
1 lemon, thinly sliced
1 clove garlic, crushed
1 lemon, thinly sliced
Paprika

Place chicken in glass or plastic bowl. Mix remaining ingredients except 1 lemon and paprika; pour over chicken. Cover and refrigerate at least 3 hours.

Remove chicken and lemon slices. Discard lemon slices; reserve marinade. Cover and grill chicken, bone sides down, 5 to 6 inches from medium coals 15 to 20 minutes; turn chicken. Cover and grill, turning and brushing 2 or 3 times with marinade, until chicken is done, 20 to 40 minutes longer.

Roll edges of remaining lemon slices in paprika; arrange around chicken. Garnish with celery leaves if desired.

6 servings

TO MICROWAVE: Prepare marinade and marinate chicken in 2-quart microwavable casserole as directed above. Remove chicken and lemon slices from marinade. Discard lemon slices; reserve marinade.

Arrange chicken, skin sides up and thickest parts to outside edge, in casserole. Cover tightly and microwave on high (100%) 12 minutes.

Place chicken, bone side down and 5 to 6 inches from medium coals, on grill. Cover and grill, turning and brushing 2 or 3 times with marinade, until done, 15 to 20 minutes.

HERBED CHICKEN

2 tablespoons margarine or butter
2 tablespoons olive or vegetable oil
¼ cup finely chopped onion
¼ cup lemon juice
2 tablespoons Worcestershire sauce
1½ teaspoons snipped fresh basil or ½ teaspoon dried basil leaves
¾ teaspoon snipped fresh oregano or ¼ teaspoon dried oregano leaves
2 large cloves garlic, finely chopped
2½- to 3-pound broiler-fryer chicken, cut up

Heat margarine and oil in rectangular pan, 13 x 9 x 2 inches, in 375° oven until margarine is melted. Stir in remaining ingredients except chicken. Place chicken, skin sides up, in pan, turning to coat with herb mixture. Bake uncovered 30 minutes. Turn chicken; bake uncovered until thickest pieces are done, about 30 minutes longer.

7 servings

TO MICROWAVE: Place margarine and oil in rectangular microwavable dish, 12 x 7½ x 2 inches. Microwave uncovered on high (100%) until margarine is melted, 45 to 60 seconds. Stir in remaining ingredients except chicken.

Place chicken in dish, turning to coat with herb mixture. Arrange chicken, skin sides up and thickest parts to outside edges, in dish. Cover with waxed paper and microwave on high (100%) 10 minutes; rotate dish ½ turn. Microwave until thickest pieces are done, 6 to 10 minutes longer.

COUSCOUS-STUFFED CHICKEN BREASTS

COUSCOUS, A MOROCCAN AND MIDDLE EASTERN STAPLE, IS MADE FROM SEMOLINA WHEAT AND HAS A RICELIKE TEXTURE. IT'S AN IDEAL BASE FOR POULTRY STUFFING, SINCE IT READILY ABSORBS THE COOKING JUICES.

2 large whole chicken breasts (about 2 pounds)
¾ cup apple-cranberry wine cooler or red wine cooler
⅔ cup couscous
⅓ cup raisins
¼ cup chopped green onions (with tops)
¼ teaspoon salt
⅛ teaspoon ground cinnamon
1 package (3 ounces) cream cheese, cut into cubes
¾ cup apple-cranberry wine cooler or red wine cooler
1 tablespoon cold water
1 teaspoon cornstarch

Remove bones from chicken breasts; cut each whole chicken breast into halves. Heat ¾ cup wine cooler to boiling in 2-quart saucepan. Stir in couscous, raisins, green onions, salt and cinnamon. Remove from heat and let stand until all wine is absorbed, 2 to 3 minutes. Stir in cream cheese. Cook and stir over low heat until cream cheese is melted.

Heat oven to 350°. Loosen skin from cut side of each chicken breast half, using a sharp knife to form a pocket. Spoon about ½ cup couscous mixture into each pocket; secure with wooden picks. Place chicken in ungreased rectangular baking dish, 12 x 7½ x 2 inches. Pour ¾ cup wine cooler over chicken. Bake uncovered until chicken is done, 35 to 40 minutes. Remove chicken to warm platter and remove wooden picks; keep chicken warm.

Pour ⅓ cup of the cooking liquid into 1-quart saucepan. Mix water and cornstarch; stir into liquid. Heat to boiling over medium heat, stirring constantly. Boil and stir 1 minute. Serve with chicken.

4 servings

CHICKEN WITH TOMATOES AND LEEKS

3 slices bacon
4 small boneless skinless chicken breast halves (about 1 pound)
2 medium leeks, cut lengthwise into halves and sliced
2 tablespoons margarine or butter
1 can (5 ounces) evaporated milk
2 teaspoons snipped fresh tarragon or ½ teaspoon dried tarragon leaves
¼ teaspoon red pepper sauce
4 Italian plum tomatoes or 2 medium tomatoes, chopped
Salt and pepper to taste

Cook bacon in 10-inch skillet until crisp; drain, reserving fat in skillet. Cook chicken breast halves in fat over medium heat, turning once, until done, 12 to 14 minutes. Remove chicken from skillet; cover and reserve. Drain fat from skillet.

Cook and stir leeks in margarine in skillet until crisp-tender, 5 to 7 minutes. Stir in milk, tarragon and red pepper sauce. Heat to boiling, stirring occasionally. Boil and stir until slightly thickened.

Crumble bacon; stir bacon, chicken and tomatoes into skillet. Heat over medium heat, spooning sauce over chicken, until chicken is hot, about 2 minutes. Sprinkle with salt and pepper.

4 servings

Couscous-stuffed Chicken Breasts

THAI CHICKEN SALAD

EXOTIC MUSHROOMS, CELLOPHANE NOODLES AND PUNGENT FRESH HERBS ARE COMBINED IN A SERRANO-SPIKED SALAD. AFTER HANDLING THE CHILE, WASH YOUR HANDS THOROUGHLY WITH SOAP AND WATER TO REMOVE EVERY TRACE OF ITS INTENSELY IRRITATING OIL.

4 small dried cloud ears or 2 pieces of dried black fungus
½ package (3¾ ounces) cellophane noodles
2 green onions (with tops), thinly sliced
1 small whole chicken breast, cooked, skinned and shredded
4 ounces medium shrimp (about 6), cooked and coarsely chopped
½ cup shredded fresh spinach
¼ cup coarsely chopped peanuts
1 tablespoon snipped mint leaves
Romaine or leaf lettuce leaves
Snipped fresh cilantro (see page 7)
Dressing (right)

Cover cloud ears with hot water. Let stand 20 minutes; drain. Cut into thin slices. Cover cellophane noodles with cold water. Let stand 10 minutes; drain. Cook noodles in boiling water until tender, about 10 minutes; drain. Cut noodles with kitchen scissors to shorten strands; cool.

Mix green onions, chicken, shrimp, spinach, peanuts and mint. Line a small platter with romaine leaves; arrange cellophane noodles on top. Spoon chicken mixture over noodles. Sprinkle with cilantro and cloud ears. Serve with Dressing.

4 servings

Thai Chicken Salad

DRESSING

¼ cup lemon juice
3 tablespoons fish sauce
2 teaspoons sugar
1 serrano chile, seeded and chopped

Mix all ingredients.

EASY CHICKEN CURRY

2 tablespoons margarine or butter
1 teaspoon curry powder
1 small onion, chopped
2 cups cut-up cooked chicken or turkey
⅓ cup raisins
1 small unpared all-purpose red apple, coarsely chopped
1 can (10¾ ounces) condensed cream of chicken soup
1 soup can water
*Hot cooked rice**
Chopped peanuts

Cook and stir margarine, curry powder and onion in 3-quart saucepan over medium heat until onion is tender, about 4 minutes.

Stir in remaining ingredients except rice and peanuts. Cook, stirring occasionally, until hot. Serve over rice; sprinkle with peanuts.

4 servings

**Stir hot, cooked green peas into rice before serving, if desired.*

GERMAN-STYLE HOT CHICKEN SALAD

THE ADDITION OF VINEGAR AND MUSTARD GIVES THIS MAIN-COURSE SALAD A SPECIAL TANG.

4 boneless skinless chicken breast halves (about 1 pound)
¼ cup vegetable oil
1 tablespoon all-purpose flour
¼ cup water
2 tablespoons white wine vinegar
2 teaspoons Dijon-style mustard
1 teaspoon dried thyme or 1 tablespoon snipped fresh thyme leaves
2 ounces mushrooms, sliced (about ¾ cup)
2 green onions (with tops), thinly sliced
Salt and pepper to taste
½ bunch romaine, torn into bite-size pieces
2 medium tomatoes, cut into wedges

Cook chicken breast halves in oil in 10-inch skillet over medium heat until done, about 6 minutes on each side. Remove chicken from skillet. Drain chicken; cool slightly. Cut into thin slices.

Stir flour into drippings in skillet. Cook over low heat, stirring constantly, until smooth and bubbly. Remove from heat; stir in water, vinegar, mustard, thyme, mushrooms and onions. Cook over low heat, stirring constantly, until mixture is bubbly. Cook and stir 1 minute. Sprinkle with salt and pepper.

Divide romaine among 4 salad plates. Arrange chicken and tomatoes on romaine; spoon mushroom mixture over top.

4 servings

GERMAN-STYLE HOT CHICKEN SALAD WITH CRACKLINS: Prepare as directed above except—substitute 2 whole chicken breasts (about 2 pounds) for the boneless skinless chicken breast halves.

Heat oven to 375°. Remove skin from chicken breasts. Place skin, fat sides down, in ungreased jelly roll pan, 15½ x 10½ x 1 inch; sprinkle with seasoned salt. Bake until crisp, about 20 minutes; drain. Cool; cut into small pieces.

Sprinkle Chicken Cracklins on salads.

WILTED SPINACH AND CHICKEN SALAD

1 boneless skinless whole chicken breast (about ½ pound)
4 slices bacon
1 tablespoon sesame seed
¼ cup vinegar
2 teaspoons sugar
1 teaspoon cornstarch
½ teaspoon salt
¼ teaspoon pepper
1 pound spinach
½ small red onion, thinly sliced

Cut chicken breast into 1-inch pieces; reserve. Cook bacon in Dutch oven over medium heat until crisp. Drain bacon, reserving fat in Dutch oven; crumble bacon and reserve. Cook and stir chicken and sesame seed in bacon fat over medium heat until chicken is white, 6 to 7 minutes.

Mix vinegar, sugar, cornstarch, salt and pepper; stir into chicken mixture. Heat to boiling, stirring constantly. Boil and stir 1 minute. Remove from heat; add spinach and onion. Toss until spinach is wilted, 2 or 3 minutes; sprinkle with bacon. Serve immediately.

4 servings

German-style Hot Chicken Salad

CHICKEN WITH LEMON GRASS

THE EXOTIC SAUCE OF THIS VIETNAMESE DISH IS FRAGRANT AND SATISFYING—SWEET, SOUR, TART AND FAINTLY SALTY, ALL AT ONCE. SKINNED AND BONED, THE MEAT COOKS QUICKLY.

6 chicken thighs (about 2 pounds)
1 stalk lemon grass, chopped (see page 7), or 3 thin strips lemon peel
*1 tablespoon fish sauce**
3 tablespoons vegetable oil
1 medium onion, sliced
2 cloves garlic, chopped
3 green onions (with tops), cut into 1-inch pieces
2 tablespoons vinegar
1 tablespoon finely chopped gingerroot (see page 7)
¼ cup water
1 tablespoon fish sauce
1 teaspoon cornstarch
1 teaspoon sugar
¼ teaspoon crushed red pepper
Hot cooked rice

Remove bones and skin from chicken thighs; cut chicken into 1-inch pieces. Mix lemon grass and 1 tablespoon fish sauce in glass or plastic bowl; stir in chicken. Cover and refrigerate at least 1 hour.

Heat oil in wok or 10-inch skillet until hot. Add sliced onion and garlic; stir-fry 1 minute. Add chicken and green onions; stir-fry 5 minutes. Reduce heat; cover and cook, stirring occasionally, 2 minutes.

Mix vinegar and gingerroot; reserve. Mix remaining ingredients except rice; stir into chicken mixture. Stir in reserved vinegar mixture. Heat to boiling, stirring constantly; cook and stir until thickened, about 1 minute. Serve with rice.

4 servings

**Fish sauce is available in Oriental specialty stores. It is also known as* Nam Pla.

SPICY CHICKEN AND BROWN RICE

THE UNEXPECTED SPICINESS OF GROUND CINNAMON AND CLOVES ADDS LIFE TO THIS MILD, CREAMY DISH.

2 cups cut-up cooked chicken or turkey
1 cup uncooked brown rice
½ cup currants or raisins
2½ cups boiling water
1 teaspoon salt
½ teaspoon ground cinnamon
¼ teaspoon ground cloves
1 small onion, chopped
1 can (10¾ ounces) condensed cream of chicken soup
Pineapple spears or spiced peaches

Heat oven to 350°. Mix all ingredients except pineapple spears in ungreased 2-quart casserole. Cover and bake 1½ hours; stir.

Cover and bake until rice is tender, 15 to 25 minutes longer. Serve with pineapple spears; sprinkle with salted nuts if desired.

6 servings

SPICY CHICKEN AND BROWN RICE IN PEPPERS: Bake chicken mixture as directed above. Cut 3 green peppers lengthwise into halves; remove seeds and membranes. Cook peppers in boiling water to cover 5 minutes; drain. Fill each pepper half with ¾ cup chicken mixture; sprinkle with salted nuts if desired.

CHICKEN CHILAQUILES CASSEROLE

New Mexico Green Sauce (below)
½ cup vegetable oil
10 flour or corn tortillas (6 to 7 inches in diameter), cut into ½-inch strips
2 cups shredded cooked chicken or turkey
2 cups shredded Chihuahua or mozzarella cheese (8 ounces)

Prepare New Mexico Green Sauce; reserve. Heat oil in 10-inch skillet until hot. Cook tortilla strips in oil until light golden brown, 30 to 60 seconds; drain on paper towels.

Heat oven to 350°. Layer half of the tortilla strips in bottom of greased 2-quart casserole; top with chicken, half of the New Mexico Green Sauce (about ⅔ cup) and 1 cup of the cheese. Gently press layers down into casserole. Repeat with remaining tortilla strips, sauce and cheese. Bake until cheese is melted and golden brown, about 30 minutes.

6 to 8 servings

NEW MEXICO GREEN SAUCE

1 large onion, finely chopped (about 1 cup)
4 poblano chiles, roasted, peeled, seeded and finely chopped (about ½ cup)
1 jalapeño chile, seeded and finely chopped
1 clove garlic, finely chopped
2 tablespoons vegetable oil
½ cup whipping cream
¼ teaspoon salt

Cook onion, chiles and garlic in oil over medium heat, stirring occasionally, until onion is tender, about 8 minutes. Stir in whipping cream and salt.

SCOTTISH-STYLE ROAST CHICKEN

THE SCOTS WERE SERVING THEIR ROAST CHICKEN WITH "SKIRLIE," A STUFFING OF OATS AND ONION, SEASONED WITH NUTMEG, CORIANDER AND GROUND BLACK PEPPER, LONG BEFORE OATS BECAME THE LATEST HEALTH-FOOD STAR.

Oat Stuffing (below)
3- to 4-pound broiler-fryer chicken
6 medium onions, cut into halves
¼ cup margarine or butter, melted

Prepare Oat Stuffing. Fill wishbone area of chicken with stuffing. Fasten neck skin to back with skewer. Fold wings across back with tips touching. Fill body cavity lightly. (Do not pack; stuffing will expand during cooking.) Tie or skewer drumsticks to tail.

Place chicken, breast side up, in shallow roasting pan. Arrange onions around chicken. Brush chicken and onions with margarine. Roast uncovered in 375° oven, brushing chicken and onions several times with remaining margarine, until chicken and onions are done, about 1½ hours.

6 servings

OAT STUFFING

1 large onion, finely chopped
¼ cup margarine or butter
1 cup regular oats
½ teaspoon salt
½ teaspoon ground coriander
¼ teaspoon pepper
⅛ teaspoon ground nutmeg

Cook and stir onion in margarine in 10-inch skillet over medium heat until light brown. Stir in remaining ingredients. Cook and stir until oats are golden brown and crisp, 3 to 4 minutes.

Cornish Hens with Corn Bread Stuffing

We most often associate sage-scented stuffing with turkey. Here, little birds get their turn for a change of pace. You may substitute a 3½-pound broiler-fryer chicken for the Cornish hens. In that case, roast uncovered at 375° for about 1¾ hours.

4 Rock Cornish hens (about 1 pound each)
½ cup chenin blanc or dry white wine
¼ cup orange juice
½ cup chopped celery
¼ cup finely chopped onion
2 tablespoons snipped parsley
¼ teaspoon ground sage
¼ teaspoon salt
⅛ teaspoon pepper
¼ cup margarine or butter
4 cups crumbled corn bread
2 tablespoons chenin blanc or dry white wine

Place Cornish hens in a large plastic bag. Pour in ½ cup wine and the orange juice. Fasten bag securely. Refrigerate at least 2 hours but no longer than 24 hours, turning bag twice. Remove hens; reserve wine mixture.

Heat oven to 375°. Cook and stir celery, onion, parsley, sage, salt and pepper in margarine in 2-quart saucepan until celery is tender; remove from heat. Stir in remaining ingredients. Spoon about 1 cup stuffing into each hen. Secure opening with skewer. Tie legs together with string. Place hens, breast sides up, on rack in shallow roasting pan. Roast uncovered, brushing with wine mixture occasionally, until thickest pieces are done, about 1 hour.

4 servings

Grilled Cornish Hens with Plum Barbecue Sauce

Plum Barbecue Sauce (below)
3 Rock Cornish hens (about 1¼ pounds each)

Prepare Plum Barbecue Sauce; reserve. Cut hens lengthwise into halves. Place bone sides down on grill. Cover and grill 5 to 6 inches from medium coals 35 minutes.

Turn hens. Cover and grill, turning and brushing with Plum Barbecue Sauce 2 or 3 times, until done, 25 to 35 minutes longer. Heat any remaining sauce and serve with hens.

6 servings

Roast Cornish Hens with Plum Barbecue Sauce: Heat oven to 350°. Place cut hens, bone sides down, on rack in shallow roasting pan. Roast uncovered 30 minutes. Brush hens generously with Plum Barbecue Sauce. Roast uncovered, brushing hens with sauce 2 or 3 times, until done, about 45 minutes longer.

Plum Barbecue Sauce

1 small onion, finely chopped (about ¼ cup)
¼ cup margarine or butter
¼ cup chile sauce
2 teaspoons Dijon-style mustard
1 can (16½ ounces) purple plums, drained, pitted and finely chopped
1 can (6 ounces) frozen lemonade concentrate, thawed

Cook onion in margarine in 2-quart saucepan, stirring occasionally, until tender, about 2 minutes. Stir in remaining ingredients.

Heat to boiling; reduce heat to low. Simmer uncovered 15 minutes, stirring occasionally.

Cornish Hens with Corn Bread Stuffing

WALNUT-STUFFED TURKEY

CHARDONNAY, A DISTINGUISHED VARIETAL WHITE WINE, BRINGS A SUBTLE FRUITINESS TO THIS WALNUT-RICH STUFFING.

3 medium onions, finely chopped
¾ cup margarine or butter
3 cups unseasoned croutons
2 cups chopped walnuts
¾ cup raisins
1 cup chardonnay or dry white wine
¼ to ½ cup water, as desired
1½ teaspoons ground sage
1¼ teaspoons salt
2 large stalks celery, chopped
10- to 12-pound turkey
2 tablespoons margarine or butter, melted
1 cup chardonnay or dry white wine
1 teaspoon instant chicken bouillon
1 cup boiling water

Cook and stir onions in ¾ cup margarine in 4-quart Dutch oven until tender; remove from heat. Stir in croutons, walnuts, raisins, 1 cup wine, ¼ to ½ cup water (depending on desired moistness of stuffing), the sage, salt and celery. Stuff turkey just before baking.

Heat oven to 325°. Place turkey, breast side up, on rack in shallow roasting pan. Brush with 2 tablespoons margarine. Pour 1 cup wine over turkey. Dissolve bouillon (dry) in 1 cup boiling water; pour over turkey. Insert meat thermometer so tip is in thickest part of inside thigh muscle or breast meat and does not touch bone.

Bake uncovered until thermometer registers 185° or until drumstick can be moved easily, 4 to 4½ hours. Place aluminum foil loosely over turkey when it begins to turn golden. When the turkey is done, remove from oven and let stand 20 minutes for easier carving.

10 servings

TURKEY TAMALE PIE

TAMALES ARE INDIVIDUALLY WRAPPED CORN HUSK PACKETS FILLED WITH SAVORY MIXTURES. THIS RECIPE FOR A "PIE" CALLS FOR ONE LARGE CORN HUSK PACKAGE, RATHER THAN A SCORE OF LITTLE ONES. THE DRY CORN HUSKS MUST BE SOFTENED FIRST. WEIGHT THEM TO KEEP THEM SUBMERGED WHILE THEY SOAK.

4 to 6 dried corn husks
Almond Red Sauce (page 89)
¾ pound cooked turkey breast, cut into ½-inch cubes (about 2 cups)
1 cup slivered almonds, toasted (see To Toast, page 25)
1 cup golden raisins
½ cup chopped red bell pepper
2 cans (4 ounces each) chopped green chiles
Tamale Dough (right)
Dairy sour cream

Rinse corn husks and remove silk; cover corn husks with warm water and let stand until softened, at least 2 hours.

Prepare Almond Red Sauce. Mix ½ cup of the sauce and the remaining ingredients except Tamale Dough and sour cream; reserve. Prepare Tamale Dough; reserve.

Heat oven to 350°. Drain corn husks; pat dry. Line greased springform pan, 10 x 3 inches, with corn husks, extending pointed ends of husks over side of pan. Spread half of the Tamale Dough over husks on bottom of pan; cover with turkey mixture. Spread remaining dough over turkey mixture up to edge of pan. Cover top of pan with piece of heavy-duty aluminum foil, 15 inches long, shaping down over side of pan (pointed ends of corn husks will bend down against outside of pan).

Bake until dough is set and slightly dry, about 1½ hours. Remove side of pan. Serve with remaining warm Almond Red Sauce and the sour cream.

8 servings

TAMALE DOUGH

2 cups instant corn flour tortilla mix
½ cup shortening
2 cups chicken broth
2 teaspoons baking powder
½ teaspoon salt

Beat all ingredients in large bowl on low speed, scraping bowl constantly, until well blended. Beat on medium speed 1 minute.

TURKEY IN JALAPEÑO CREAM SAUCE

Jalapeño Cream Sauce (right)
2 large boneless, skinless turkey breasts (about 1 pound each), each cut into 3 slices
¼ cup all-purpose flour
½ teaspoon cracked black pepper
¼ teaspoon salt
¼ cup margarine or butter

Prepare Jalapeño Cream Sauce; reserve. Flatten each turkey breast slice to ¼-inch thickness between plastic wrap or waxed paper.

Mix flour, pepper and salt. Coat turkey with flour mixture. Heat margarine in 10-inch skillet until melted. Cook turkey in margarine, turning once, until done, about 8 minutes. Serve with Jalapeño Cream Sauce.

6 servings

JALAPEÑO CREAM SAUCE

1 to 2 jalapeño chiles, seeded and finely chopped
1 clove garlic, finely chopped
2 teaspoons vegetable oil
1 container (10 ounces) crème fraîche or Quick Crème Fraîche (below)
⅛ teaspoon salt
Dash of pepper

Cook chiles and garlic in oil over low heat, stirring frequently, until tender, about 4 minutes. Remove from heat; stir in remaining ingredients.

QUICK CRÈME FRAÎCHE

⅓ cup whipping cream
⅔ cup sour cream

Gradually stir whipping cream into sour cream. Cover and refrigerate up to 48 hours.

GLAZED TURKEY TENDERLOINS

2 turkey breast tenderloins (about 1 pound)
1 tablespoon vegetable oil
⅓ cup orange marmalade
1 teaspoon finely chopped gingerroot (see page 7) or ½ teaspoon ground ginger
1 teaspoon Worcestershire sauce

Cook turkey breast tenderloins in oil in 10-inch skillet over medium heat until brown on one side, about 5 minutes; turn turkey. Stir in remaining ingredients; reduce heat.

Cover and simmer, stirring occasionally, until turkey is done and sauce is thickened, about 15 minutes. Cut turkey into thin slices; spoon sauce over turkey.

4 servings

DUCK WITH PINE NUT WILD RICE

Apricot Basting Sauce (right)
4½- to 5-pound duckling
Pine Nut Wild Rice (below)

Prepare Apricot Basting Sauce. Heat oven to 350°. Place duckling, breast side up, on rack in shallow roasting pan. Brush with Apricot Basting Sauce. Insert meat thermometer so tip is in thickest part of inside thigh muscle and does not touch bone. Do not add water. Do not cover.

Roast, brushing with sauce 2 or 3 times, until thermometer registers 180° to 185° or drumstick meat feels very soft when pressed between fingers, 2 to 2½ hours. Serve with Pine Nut Wild Rice.

4 servings

PINE NUT WILD RICE

½ cup uncooked wild rice
2 tablespoons sliced green onions (with tops)
1 teaspoon margarine or butter
1½ cups chicken broth
½ cup pine nuts, toasted (see To Toast, page 25) (2 ounces)
½ cup chopped dried pears
½ cup currants

Cook and stir wild rice and onions in margarine in 2-quart heavy saucepan over medium heat until onions are tender, about 3 minutes. Stir in broth. Heat to boiling, stirring occasionally; reduce heat. Cover and simmer until wild rice is tender, 40 to 50 minutes. Stir in pine nuts, pears and currants.

APRICOT BASTING SAUCE

½ cup apricot jam
¼ cup dried apricots, finely chopped
¼ cup dry white wine
1 tablespoon honey
1 teaspoon Worcestershire sauce

Heat all ingredients over low heat, stirring occasionally, until jam is melted.

COMPANY POT ROAST

*3- to 4-pound beef rolled rump roast**
3 tablespoons vegetable oil
¾ cup sour cream
¾ cup dry red wine
½ teaspoon salt
½ teaspoon pepper
½ teaspoon dried thyme leaves
2 cloves garlic, finely chopped
2 medium carrots, cut crosswise into 1-inch pieces
2 medium onions, sliced and separated into rings
½ cup water
2 tablespoons all-purpose flour
1 tablespoon lemon juice

Cook beef in oil in ovenproof Dutch oven until brown; remove beef. Mix remaining ingredients except water, flour and lemon juice in Dutch oven.

Return beef to Dutch oven. Cover and bake in 325° oven until beef is tender, about 3½ hours. Remove beef and vegetables to heated platter; keep warm while preparing gravy.

Skim fat from liquid. Shake water and flour in tightly covered container; gradually stir into liquid. Heat to boiling, stirring constantly. Boil and stir 1 minute. Stir in lemon juice; cook 1 minute. Slice beef thinly; serve with gravy.

10 servings

TO MICROWAVE: Omit oil; increase flour to 3 tablespoons. Place 3-pound beef roast in 3-quart microwavable casserole. Cover tightly and microwave on high (100%) 12 minutes; drain.

Mix remaining ingredients except water, flour and lemon juice; add to casserole, spooning some of mixture over beef. Cover tightly and microwave 10 minutes; rotate casserole ½ turn. Microwave on medium-low (30%) 1 hour; turn beef over. Cover tightly and microwave until beef is tender, 45 minutes to 1 hour longer. Remove beef and vegetables to heated platter; keep warm.

Mix water and flour and stir into liquid as directed above. Microwave uncovered on high (100%) 2 minutes; stir in lemon juice. Microwave uncovered until thickened, 1 to 2 minutes longer. Serve beef as directed above.

**Beef bottom round or boneless chuck eye roast can be substituted for the rolled rump roast.*

CHORIZO-STUFFED BEEF ROAST

THIS IS A SUCCULENT ROAST STUFFED WITH SPICY SAUSAGE AND BRAISED IN A SAVORY TOMATO SAUCE: A CLASSIC FROM LATIN AMERICA. CHORIZO IS A CHILE-SPIKED FAVORITE IN THE DOMINICAN REPUBLIC.

3-pound beef boneless eye of round roast or rolled rump roast
½ pound bulk chorizo or Italian sausage
2 tablespoons olive or vegetable oil
1 medium onion, chopped
3 cloves garlic, finely chopped
1 large green pepper, coarsely chopped
1 teaspoon dried oregano leaves
1 teaspoon salt
¼ teaspoon pepper
2 bay leaves
1 can (8 ounces) tomato sauce

Cut a narrow (1-inch) X shape all the way through beef roast with long, thin, sharp knife. Fill X cuts with sausage. Heat oil in Dutch oven until hot. Cook beef over medium heat until brown on all sides, about 15 minutes; drain fat.

Add remaining ingredients. Heat to boiling; reduce heat. Cover and simmer until beef is tender, 2 to 2½ hours.

Remove bay leaves. Slice beef; arrange on platter. Skim fat from sauce. Pour some of the sauce over beef. Serve beef with remaining sauce and hot cooked black beans or rice if desired.

8 to 10 servings

MEXICAN GRILLED STEAK

2 high-quality beef flank steaks (1 to 1½ pounds each)
Juice of 2 limes (about ½ cup)
4 cloves garlic, crushed
⅓ cup snipped fresh oregano or 2 tablespoons dried oregano leaves
2 tablespoons olive or vegetable oil
2 teaspoons salt
½ teaspoon pepper

Place beef steaks in shallow glass or plastic dish. Mix remaining ingredients; pour over beef. Cover and refrigerate at least 8 hours but no longer than 24 hours, turning beef occasionally.

Cover and grill beef 4 to 5 inches from medium coals, turning once, until of desired doneness, 10 to 15 minutes for medium. Cut beef across grain at slanted angle into thin slices. Serve with tortillas and guacamole if desired.

8 servings

TO BROIL: Marinate beef steaks as directed above. Set oven control to broil. Place beef on rack in broiler pan. Broil with tops 2 to 3 inches from heat until brown, about 5 minutes. Turn beef; broil 5 minutes longer. Cut and serve as directed above.

Mexican Grilled Steak

THREE-MEAT STEW

FROM FINLAND COMES A STEW THAT REFLECTS THE RUSSIAN INFLUENCE ON ITS EASTERN BORDER. HERE THE FLAVORS OF BEEF, LAMB AND PORK ARE ENHANCED WITH SIMPLE SEASONINGS AND BOILED POTATOES. IN FINLAND THIS DISH WOULD COOK OVERNIGHT. OUR RECIPE PRODUCES THE SAME SUCCULENT STEW IN A COUPLE OF HOURS.

1 pound beef boneless chuck or round
1 pound lamb boneless shoulder
1 pound pork boneless shoulder
2 tablespoons all-purpose flour
¾ teaspoon salt
½ teaspoon pepper
½ teaspoon ground allspice
2 large onions, sliced
1 bay leaf
1½ cups hot water
Boiled potatoes

Heat oven to 350°. Trim fat from meats; cut meats into 1-inch cubes. Toss meats, flour, salt, pepper and allspice. Alternate layers of meat and onions in Dutch oven. Add bay leaf. Pour hot water over meat and onion mixture. Cover and cook 2½ hours.

Uncover and cook, stirring occasionally, until meat is tender and broth is slightly thickened, about 30 minutes. Remove bay leaf. Serve with potatoes.

8 servings

CRUSHED PEPPER BEEF KABOBS

THESE KABOBS ARE NOT FOR TIMID TASTE BUDS! THIS RECIPE IS A TWIST ON THE TRADITIONAL FRENCH FAVORITE STEAK AU POIVRE. YOU CAN GRILL THEM OVER CHARCOAL, TOO.

1½ pounds beef boneless round, tip or chuck steak
½ cup zinfandel or dry red wine
1 tablespoon olive or vegetable oil
½ teaspoon salt
1 clove garlic, cut into halves
2 tablespoons prepared mustard
2 tablespoons black peppercorns, coarsely crushed
2 small onions, cut lengthwise into fourths
2 small zucchini, cut into 1-inch slices
1 red or yellow bell pepper, cut into 1-inch pieces
4 mushrooms
Olive oil

Trim excess fat from beef steak; cut beef into 1-inch cubes. Place in glass or plastic bowl. Mix wine, 1 tablespoon oil, the salt and garlic; pour over beef. Cover and refrigerate at least 6 hours but no longer than 24 hours, stirring occasionally.

Remove beef; drain thoroughly. Thread beef cubes on four 11-inch metal skewers, leaving space between cubes. Brush with mustard; sprinkle with peppercorns.

Set oven control to broil. Place kabobs on rack in broiler pan. Broil with tops about 3 inches from heat 5 minutes; turn over. Broil 5 minutes longer.

Alternate onion, zucchini, bell pepper and mushrooms on each of four 11-inch metal skewers, leaving space between each. Place kabobs on rack in broiler pan with beef. Turn beef; brush vegetables with oil. Broil kabobs, turning and brushing vegetables with oil, until beef is done and vegetables are crisp-tender, 5 to 6 minutes.

4 servings

TEXAS RED CHILI

TEXAS RED MEANS CHILI TO A LOT OF PEOPLE, BUT FOLKS DEBATE THE ADDITION OF TOMATO IN ANY FORM.

3 pounds beef boneless round steak, cut into 1-inch cubes
1 large onion, finely chopped (about 1 cup)
4 cloves garlic, finely chopped
¼ cup vegetable oil
2 cups tomato purée
2 to 3 tablespoons ground red chiles
1 teaspoon cumin seed, ground
1 teaspoon ground coriander
4 Anaheim chiles, seeded and chopped
4 jalapeño chiles, seeded and chopped
Shredded Cheddar cheese
Flour tortillas
Cooked pinto beans

Cook and stir beef, onion and garlic in oil in Dutch oven until beef is brown. Stir in remaining ingredients except cheese, tortillas and beans.

Heat to boiling; reduce heat. Cover and simmer, stirring occasionally, until beef is tender, about 2 hours. Serve with cheese, tortillas and beans.

6 servings (about 1¼ cups each)

Crushed Pepper Beef Kabobs
FOLLOWING PAGES: Texas Red Chili, White Bean Chili (page 33) and Vegetable Cornmeal Muffins (page 139)

GREETINGS
OF THE GREAT
You From

BEEF TORTILLA CASSEROLE

Basic Red Sauce (below)
Southwest Guacamole (right)
½ cup vegetable oil
10 corn tortillas (6 to 7 inches in diameter), cut into 2-inch-wide strips
1 pound ground beef
2 Anaheim chiles, seeded and finely chopped
1 medium onion, chopped (about ½ cup)
1 can (15 ounces) pinto beans, drained
2 cups shredded Cheddar cheese (8 ounces)
Sour cream

Prepare Basic Red Sauce and Southwest Guacamole; reserve. Heat oil in 10-inch skillet until hot. Cook tortilla strips in oil until light golden brown, about 1 minute; drain. Cook and stir ground beef, chiles and onion until beef is brown; drain.

Heat oven to 350°. Arrange tortilla strips in greased rectangular baking dish, 13 x 9 x 2 inches. Top with beef mixture, Basic Red Sauce, beans and cheese. Bake until hot and bubbly, 25 to 30 minutes. Serve with Southwest Guacamole and sour cream.

8 servings

BASIC RED SAUCE

8 ancho chiles
3½ cups warm water
1 medium onion, chopped (about ½ cup)
2 cloves garlic, chopped
¼ cup vegetable oil
1 can (8 ounces) tomato sauce
1 tablespoon dried oregano leaves
1 tablespoon cumin seed
1 teaspoon salt

Cover chiles with warm water. Let stand until softened, about 30 minutes; drain. Strain liquid; reserve. Remove stems, seeds and membranes from chiles.

Cook and stir onion and garlic in oil in 2-quart saucepan until onion is tender. Stir in chiles, 2 cups of the reserved liquid and the remaining ingredients. Heat to boiling; reduce heat. Simmer uncovered 20 minutes; cool.

Pour into food processor workbowl fitted with steel blade or into blender container; cover and process until smooth. Cover and refrigerate up to 10 days.

SOUTHWEST GUACAMOLE

5 ripe avocados, peeled and pitted
4 cloves garlic, finely chopped
1 medium tomato, chopped (about 1 cup)
¼ cup lime juice
½ teaspoon salt

Mash avocados until slightly lumpy. Stir in remaining ingredients. Cover and refrigerate 1 hour.

BAKED CHIMICHANGAS

Almond Red Sauce (see page 89)
Jalapeño Cream Sauce (see page 79)
1 pound ground beef
1 small onion, finely chopped (about ¼ cup)
1 clove garlic, finely chopped
¼ cup slivered almonds
¼ cup raisins
1 tablespoon red wine vinegar
1 teaspoon ground red chiles
½ teaspoon salt
¼ teaspoon ground cinnamon
⅛ teaspoon ground cloves
1 can (4 ounces) chopped green chiles
1 medium tomato, chopped (about 1 cup)
8 flour tortillas (10 inches in diameter), warmed
1 egg, beaten
2 tablespoons margarine or butter, softened

Prepare Almond Red Sauce and Jalapeño Cream Sauce; reserve. Cook and stir ground beef, onion and garlic in 10-inch skillet over medium heat until beef is brown; drain.

Stir in remaining ingredients except tortillas, egg and margarine. Heat to boiling; reduce heat. Simmer uncovered 20 minutes, stirring occasionally.

Heat oven to 500°. Spoon about ½ cup beef mixture onto center of each tortilla. Fold one end of tortilla up about 1 inch over beef mixture; fold right and left sides over folded end, overlapping. Fold remaining end down; brush edges with egg to seal. Brush each chimichanga with margarine.

Place seam sides down in ungreased jelly roll pan, 15½ x 10½ x 1 inch. Bake until tortillas begin to brown and filling is hot, 8 to 10 minutes. Serve with Almond Red Sauce and Jalapeño Cream Sauce.

4 servings

ALMOND RED SAUCE

½ cup slivered almonds, toasted (see To Toast, page 25)
1 large onion, finely chopped (about 1 cup)
1 clove garlic, crushed
2 tablespoons vegetable oil
1 can (8 ounces) tomato sauce
2 teaspoons paprika
1 teaspoon ground red chiles
¼ teaspoon ground red pepper

Place almonds in food processor workbowl fitted with steel blade or in blender container; cover and process until finely ground.

Cook onion and garlic in oil over medium heat, stirring frequently, until onion is tender. Stir in remaining ingredients except almonds.

Heat to boiling; reduce heat. Simmer 1 minute, stirring constantly; stir in almonds. Serve hot.

FRIED CHIMICHANGAS: Omit 2 tablespoons margarine or butter. Heat vegetable oil (about 1 inch) to 365°. Fry chimichangas, 2 or 3 at a time, in oil, turning once, until golden brown, 3 to 4 minutes. Keep warm in 300° oven.

BAKED STUFFED PAPAYAS

THE HAWAIIAN PAPAYA FOUND IN MOST AMERICAN MARKETS IS SOMETIMES SWEETER THAN ITS SOUTH-OF-THE-BORDER COUSIN.

1 pound ground beef
1 medium onion, chopped
1 clove garlic, finely chopped
1 can (16 ounces) whole tomatoes, drained
1 jalapeño chile, finely chopped
½ teaspoon salt
¼ teaspoon pepper
4 papayas (about 12 ounces each)
2 tablespoons grated Parmesan cheese

Cook and stir beef, onion and garlic in 10-inch skillet over medium heat until beef is light brown; drain. Stir in tomatoes, jalapeño chile, salt and pepper; break up tomatoes with fork. Heat to boiling; reduce heat. Simmer uncovered until most of the liquid is evaporated, about 10 minutes.

Heat oven to 350°. Cut papayas lengthwise into halves; remove seeds. Place about ⅓ cup beef mixture in each papaya half; sprinkle with cheese. Arrange in shallow roasting pan. Pour very hot water into pan to within 1 inch of tops of papaya halves. Cook uncovered until papayas are very tender and hot, about 30 minutes.

4 servings

Peach-glazed Pork Roast

The marinade for this juicy roast recalls many of the same flavors to be found in a jar of chutney: garlic, mustard, peach and citrus.

4-pound pork boneless top loin roast
1½ cups peach-flavored wine cooler
1 tablespoon snipped fresh rosemary or 1 teaspoon dried rosemary leaves, crushed
1 teaspoon salt
1 teaspoon dry mustard
1 teaspoon finely shredded lemon peel
2 cloves garlic, crushed
½ cup peach preserves
1 tablespoon cold water
1 teaspoon cornstarch

Place pork roast in shallow glass or plastic dish. Mix wine cooler, rosemary, salt, mustard, lemon peel and garlic; pour over pork. Cover and refrigerate, turning occasionally, at least 12 hours.

Heat oven to 325°. Place pork, fat side up, on rack in shallow roasting pan. Insert meat thermometer so tip is in center of the thickest part of pork and does not rest in fat. Pour wine cooler mixture over pork. Bake uncovered 1½ hours, spooning pan drippings over pork occasionally.

Spoon peach preserves over pork. Bake until thermometer registers 170°, about 1 hour longer. Remove pork and rack from pan; keep pork warm. Pour pan drippings into 1-quart saucepan; heat to boiling. Mix water and cornstarch; stir into pan drippings. Heat to boiling, stirring constantly. Boil and stir 1 minute. Serve with pork.

12 servings

Pork Tenderloin with Apples

Tenderloin is aptly named; delicate and practically fat-free, it needs only brief cooking when sliced thin.

1½ pounds pork tenderloin
1 tablespoon margarine or butter
1 tablespoon vegetable oil
Salt and pepper to taste
8 ounces mushrooms, sliced
2 unpared cooking apples, cut into cubes
½ cup whipping cream
¼ cup apple cider or chicken broth
1 tablespoon Dijon-style mustard

Cut pork tenderloin diagonally into ¼-inch slices. Cook a few slices pork at a time in margarine and oil in 10-inch skillet over medium heat until light brown on both sides. Sprinkle with salt and pepper. Remove pork; keep warm.

Cook mushrooms and apples in skillet, stirring occasionally, until tender and liquid is evaporated. Stir in remaining ingredients. Heat to boiling, stirring constantly. Pour over pork. Sprinkle with snipped parsley if desired.

6 servings

Peach-glazed Pork Roast

Cranberry Pork Chops with Rosemary

4 pork loin or rib chops, about 1 inch thick
1 tablespoon vegetable oil
1 tablespoon snipped fresh rosemary or 1 teaspoon dried rosemary leaves, crushed
½ teaspoon salt
1 medium onion, sliced and separated into rings
1 cup French colombard or dry white wine
¼ cup packed brown sugar
½ package (12-ounce size) fresh or frozen cranberries (about 1½ cups)

Cook pork chops in oil in 10-inch skillet over medium heat until brown on both sides, about 20 minutes; drain. Sprinkle with rosemary and salt. Arrange onion on pork; pour wine into skillet. Heat to boiling; reduce heat. Cover and simmer until pork is done, 30 to 45 minutes. Remove pork to warm platter; keep warm.

Heat liquid in skillet to boiling; boil until thickened and reduced by half. Stir in brown sugar and cranberries. Heat to boiling; reduce heat. Cover and boil gently until cranberries pop, about 5 minutes. Serve over pork. Garnish with fresh rosemary if desired.

4 servings

Broiled Pork Chops and Onions

4 pork loin or rib chops, each about ¾-inch thick
2 medium onions
Salt to taste
Rubbed sage to taste
About 2 teaspoons margarine or butter, melted
Pepper to taste

Set oven control to broil. Place pork chops on rack in broiler pan. Broil with tops 3 to 5 inches from heat until pork is light brown, about 10 minutes. Turn pork.

Cut ¼-inch slice from both ends of each onion. Cut onions crosswise into halves; place in broiler pan with pork. Sprinkle salt and sage over onions. Broil until onions are light brown, about 5 minutes; turn onions. Sprinkle with salt and sage; drizzle with margarine. Broil until pork is done, about 5 minutes longer. Sprinkle salt and pepper over pork.

4 servings

To Grill: Grill pork and onions 4 inches from medium coals, turning 1 or 2 times and brushing onions with margarine, until pork is done (170°), about 20 minutes. Sprinkle salt and sage over onions; sprinkle salt and pepper over pork.

Broiled Pork Chops and Onions

GRILLED PORK TACOS

Papaya Relish (right)
1 tablespoon margarine or butter
1 pound pork boneless center loin roast, cut into 2 x ¼-inch strips
½ cup chopped fresh papaya (see page 7)
½ cup chopped fresh pineapple
10 flour tortillas (6 to 7 inches in diameter), warmed
1½ cups shredded Monterey Jack cheese (6 ounces)
2 tablespoons margarine or butter, melted

Prepare Papaya Relish; reserve. Heat 1 tablespoon margarine in 10-inch skillet over medium heat until hot and bubbly. Cook pork in margarine, stirring occasionally, until no longer pink, about 10 minutes; drain. Stir in papaya and pineapple. Heat, stirring occasionally, until hot.

Heat oven to 425°. Spoon about ¼ cup pork mixture onto half of each tortilla; top with about 2 tablespoons cheese. Fold tortillas into halves. Arrange five assembled tacos in ungreased jelly roll pan, 15½ x 10½ x 1 inch; brush with melted margarine. Bake until light golden brown, about 10 minutes. Repeat with remaining tacos. Serve with Papaya Relish and, if desired, sour cream.

5 servings

Grilled Pork Tacos

PAPAYA RELISH

PAPAYA RELISH IS DELICIOUS WITH SIMPLE GRILLED MEATS, TOO.

½ cup chopped red onion
½ cup chopped red bell pepper
1 small red chile, seeded and finely chopped
1 tablespoon vegetable oil
¼ cup snipped fresh mint leaves
2 tablespoons lime juice
1 papaya (see page 7), pared, seeded and cut into ½-inch cubes

Cook onion, bell pepper and chile in oil over medium heat, stirring frequently, until tender. Stir in remaining ingredients. Cover and refrigerate until chilled, about 2 hours.

Szechuan-style Pork

1 pound pork boneless loin or leg
1 tablespoon soy sauce
2 teaspoons cornstarch
½ teaspoon ground red pepper
1 clove garlic, finely chopped
2 tablespoons vegetable oil
3 cups broccoli flowerets or 1 package (16 ounces) frozen broccoli cuts, thawed
2 small onions, cut into eighths
1 can (8 ounces) whole water chestnuts, drained
¼ cup chicken broth
½ cup peanuts
Hot cooked rice

Cut pork into slices, 2 x 1 x ⅛ inch. Toss pork, soy sauce, cornstarch, red pepper and garlic in glass or plastic bowl. Cover and refrigerate 20 minutes.

Heat 12-inch skillet or wok until 1 or 2 drops of water bubble and skitter when sprinkled in skillet.

Add oil; rotate skillet to coat bottom. Add pork; cook and stir until no longer pink. Add broccoli, onions and water chestnuts; cook and stir 2 minutes. Stir in broth; heat to boiling. Stir in peanuts. Serve with rice.

4 servings

To Microwave: Increase cornstarch to 1 tablespoon. Omit oil. Cut pork as directed above. Toss pork, soy sauce, cornstarch, red pepper and garlic in 3-quart microwavable casserole. Cover tightly and refrigerate for 20 minutes. Microwave tightly covered on high (100%) 4 minutes; stir. Cover tightly and microwave until no longer pink, 5 to 6 minutes longer.

Stir in broccoli, onions, water chestnuts and broth. Cover tightly and microwave 3 minutes; stir. Cover tightly and microwave until broccoli is crisp-tender, 3 to 4 minutes. Stir in peanuts.

Baked Spareribs with Spicy Barbecue Sauce

4½-pound rack fresh pork loin back ribs, cut into serving pieces
Spicy Barbecue Sauce (below)

Heat oven to 325°. Place pork ribs meaty sides up, on rack in shallow roasting pan. Roast uncovered 1½ hours.

Prepare Spicy Barbecue Sauce. Brush with Spicy Barbecue Sauce. Roast, turning and brushing frequently with sauce, until done, about 45 minutes longer. Serve with remaining sauce.

6 servings

To Grill: Place pork ribs in Dutch oven; add 3 cups water. Heat to boiling; reduce heat. Cover and simmer 5 minutes; drain. Cover and grill pork 5 to 6 inches from medium coals, brushing with Spicy Barbecue Sauce every 3 minutes, until done and meat begins to pull away from bones (170°), 15 to 20 minutes.

Spicy Barbecue Sauce

⅓ cup margarine or butter
2 tablespoons vinegar
2 tablespoons water
1 teaspoon sugar
½ teaspoon garlic powder
½ teaspoon onion powder
½ teaspoon pepper
Dash of ground red pepper

Heat all ingredients, stirring frequently, until margarine is melted.

HAM WITH APPLES AND PEARS

SWEET FRUIT AND SALTY HAM ARE A PERFECT MATCH ENHANCED WITH MUSTARD, BROWN SUGAR AND CLOVES.

¼ cup packed brown sugar
1 tablespoon cornstarch
⅛ teaspoon ground cloves
1 cup white zinfandel or rosé wine
1 tablespoon prepared mustard
1 fully cooked smoked ham slice, 1 inch thick (about 2 pounds)
2 unpared all-purpose apples, cut crosswise into 1-inch slices
2 unpared pears, cut crosswise into 1-inch slices

Mix brown sugar, cornstarch and cloves in 1-quart saucepan. Stir in wine and mustard. Heat to boiling, stirring constantly. Boil and stir 1 minute.

Set oven control to broil. Place ham slice on rack in broiler pan; arrange apples and pears around ham. Broil with top about 3 inches from heat until ham is light brown, about 10 minutes. Turn ham, apples and pears; broil until ham is light brown, about 6 minutes longer. Brush ham, apples and pears with wine sauce during last 2 minutes of broiling. Serve with remaining sauce.

6 servings

VEAL CHOPS WITH BROWNED ONIONS

1 tablespoon margarine or butter
1 tablespoon vegetable oil
4 veal rib chops, each about ¾ inch thick
½ package (16-ounce size) frozen small whole onions
2 small zucchini, cut into ½-inch pieces
Salt and pepper to taste

Heat margarine and oil in 10-inch skillet until margarine is melted. Arrange veal chops and onions in skillet. Cook uncovered over medium heat, turning onions frequently, until veal is brown, about 7 minutes.

Turn veal; add zucchini. Cover and cook until onions and zucchini are tender, about 5 minutes. Sprinkle with salt and pepper.

4 servings

VEAL PATTIES WITH PEARS

1 pound ground veal
¼ cup butter cracker crumbs (about 6 round crackers)
¾ teaspoon ground allspice
½ teaspoon salt
¼ teaspoon pepper
1 egg
1 tablespoon margarine or butter
¼ cup slivered almonds
2 small firm unpared pears, cut into ½-inch slices
1 cup apple juice
2 teaspoons cornstarch

Mix ground veal, cracker crumbs, allspice, salt, pepper and egg. Shape into 4 patties, each about ¾ inch thick. Heat margarine in 10-inch skillet over medium heat until melted. Cook patties in margarine, turning once, until brown and no longer pink in center, 7 to 8 minutes on each side. Remove patties; keep warm.

Add almonds and pears to skillet. Mix apple juice and cornstarch until smooth; stir into skillet. Heat to boiling, stirring constantly. Boil and stir 1 minute. Pour sauce and pears over veal.

4 servings

TURKEY PATTIES WITH PEARS: Substitute 1 pound ground turkey for the veal.

Pecan-Breaded Lamb Chops

These chops are irresistible. The mustard coating is a piquant French touch that holds the crusty nut coating in place and ensures juicy meat.

1 egg white
1 tablespoon Dijon-style mustard
½ cup finely chopped pecans
½ cup soft bread crumbs (about 1⅓ slices bread)
1 clove garlic, finely chopped
6 lamb loin or shoulder chops, about ¾ inch thick
2 tablespoons vegetable oil
2 tablespoons brandy

Beat egg white slightly in small bowl; stir in mustard. Mix pecans, bread crumbs and garlic. Dip lamb chops into mustard mixture; coat with pecan mixture.

Heat oil in 10-inch skillet until hot. Cook lamb in oil over low heat until deep golden brown, about 10 minutes on each side. Remove from heat; immediately sprinkle brandy around lamb in skillet.

6 servings

Lamb Tagine with Dates

In Morocco, this fragrantly spiced lamb casserole would be served in an ornate domed serving dish known as a tagine. Couscous would be presented as an accompaniment.

3 pounds lamb boneless shoulder
2 tablespoons olive or vegetable oil
1 large onion, chopped
2 cloves garlic, finely chopped
1 teaspoon salt
½ teaspoon coarsely ground pepper
½ teaspoon ground cinnamon
¼ teaspoon saffron
2 cups water
1 tablespoon honey
1 cup whole pitted dates
Toasted almonds (see To Toast, page 25)
Lemon slices

Trim fat from lamb; cut lamb into 1-inch cubes. Heat oil in Dutch oven until hot. Cook and stir lamb in oil until all liquid is evaporated and lamb is brown, about 25 minutes; drain.

Stir in onion, garlic, salt, pepper, cinnamon and saffron; cook and stir over medium heat 5 minutes. Stir in water and honey. Heat to boiling; reduce heat. Cover and simmer, stirring occasionally, until lamb is tender, 1½ to 2 hours.

Stir dates into lamb mixture; simmer uncovered 5 minutes. Spoon onto platter. Garnish with almonds and lemon slices. Serve with couscous if desired.

8 servings

Green Chile Stew

SUBSTITUTE ANAHEIM CHILES FOR THE POBLANO CHILES TO MODERATE THE "HEAT" OF THE DISH. THIS IS A VERY FRAGRANT STEW, RICH WITH THE FLAVOR OF LAMB AND THE ACCENTS OF LEMON PEEL AND JUNIPER BERRIES.

3 pounds lamb boneless shoulder
1 large onion, chopped (about 1 cup)
3 cloves garlic, finely chopped
¼ cup vegetable oil
2 cups chicken broth
1 teaspoon salt
1 teaspoon dried juniper berries, crushed
¾ teaspoon pepper
1 tablespoon all-purpose flour
¼ cup water
4 medium poblano chiles, roasted, peeled, seeded and cut into 2 x ¼-inch strips
2 tablespoons finely shredded lemon peel

Trim excess fat from lamb; cut lamb into 1-inch cubes. Cook and stir lamb, onion and garlic in oil in Dutch oven until lamb is no longer pink; drain.

Stir in broth, salt, juniper berries and pepper. Heat to boiling; reduce heat. Cover and simmer, stirring occasionally, until lamb is tender, about 1 hour.

Shake flour and water in tightly covered container; stir into lamb mixture. Heat to boiling, stirring constantly. Boil and stir 1 minute. Stir in chiles. Sprinkle each serving with lemon peel.

4 servings (about 1¼ cups each)

Lamb Patties with Summer Squash

1 pound ground lamb
½ teaspoon garlic salt
¼ teaspoon pepper
2 small onions, cut into fourths
1 small green pepper, cut into 1-inch pieces
1 small summer squash, cut into ½-inch slices
1 tablespoon snipped fresh marjoram or 1 teaspoon dried marjoram leaves

Mix lamb, garlic, salt and pepper. Shape into 4 patties, each about ½ inch thick. Cook patties in 10-inch skillet over medium heat until light brown, about 5 minutes; turn.

Arrange onions, green pepper and squash around patties; sprinkle with marjoram. Cover and cook until lamb is done and vegetables are crisp-tender, about 8 minutes.

4 servings

TO MICROWAVE: Prepare and shape lamb patties as directed above. Arrange patties on microwavable rack. Cover with waxed paper and microwave on high (100%) 4 minutes.

Arrange vegetables on and around lamb; sprinkle with marjoram. Cover with waxed paper and microwave 4 minutes; rotate rack ½ turn. Microwave until vegetables are crisp-tender and lamb is done, 3 to 5 minutes longer.

Ground Lamb Kabobs

THESE SPICED MINCED-MEAT KABOBS ARE GRILLED ON SKEWERS, THEN TUCKED INTO POCKET BREAD FOR SERVING.

6 pocket breads
1½ pounds ground lamb
1 medium onion, chopped
1 cup snipped parsley leaves
1¼ teaspoons salt
½ teaspoon coarsely ground pepper
½ teaspoon ground cumin
½ teaspoon paprika
¼ teaspoon ground nutmeg
Vegetable oil
2 medium tomatoes, chopped
4 green onions (with tops), sliced
Plain yogurt

Split pocket breads and keep warm in the oven. Place lamb, chopped onion, parsley, salt, pepper, cumin, paprika and nutmeg in food processor workbowl fitted with steel blade; cover and process with about 20 on/off motions until mixture forms a paste.

Divide lamb mixture into 12 equal parts. Shape each part into a roll, 5 x 1 inch. (For easy shaping, dip hands in cold water from time to time.) Place 2 rolls lengthwise on each of six 14-inch metal skewers. Brush kabobs with oil.

Grill kabobs about 4 inches from medium coals, turning 2 or 3 times, until no longer pink inside, 10 to 12 minutes. Remove kabobs from skewers; serve on pocket bread halves topped with tomatoes, green onions and yogurt.

6 servings

Grilled Jalapeño Buffalo Burgers

Hot Chile Sauce (below)
1½ pounds ground buffalo or ground beef
1 medium onion, finely chopped (about ½ cup)
2 to 3 jalapeño chiles, seeded and finely chopped
1 clove garlic, finely chopped

Prepare Hot Chile Sauce; reserve. Mix remaining ingredients. Shape mixture into 6 patties, each about ½ inch thick.

Brush grill with vegetable oil. Grill patties about 4 inches from medium coals, turning once, until of desired doneness, 4 to 6 minutes on each side for medium. Serve with Hot Chile Sauce.

6 servings

BROILED JALAPEÑO BUFFALO BURGERS: Set oven control to broil. Place patties on rack in broiler pan. Broil with tops about 3 inches from heat, turning once, until of desired doneness, 4 to 6 minutes on each side for medium.

Hot Chile Sauce

2 cups water
6 to 8 dried cascabel chiles or ½ medium ancho chile
¼ cup red wine vinegar
1 teaspoon dry mustard
1 clove garlic
¼ cup olive oil

Heat water to boiling; stir in chiles. Boil uncovered 5 minutes; drain. Remove stems.

Place chiles, vinegar, mustard and garlic in blender container; cover and blend until chiles are finely chopped. Gradually pour in oil, blending until smooth.

Ground Lamb Kabobs

RABBIT STEWED IN STOUT

THE ALCOHOL IN THE IRISH STOUT EVAPORATES WHILE THE FULLNESS OF ITS FLAVOR REMAINS. SERVE THIS HEARTY BACON-SCENTED STEW WITH PARSLEYED POTATOES OR EGG NOODLES. SERVE STOUT OR, IF PREFERRED, RED WINE.

4 slices bacon
½ cup all-purpose flour
1 teaspoon salt
¼ teaspoon pepper
¼ teaspoon paprika
3- to 3½-pound rabbit, cut up
8 ounces mushrooms, cut into halves
1 jar (16 ounces) whole onions, drained
½ teaspoon dried thyme leaves
1 bay leaf
1 bottle (12 ounces) Irish stout or dark beer
2 tablespoons cold water
1 tablespoon cornstarch
Snipped parsley

Fry bacon in Dutch oven until crisp. Remove bacon and reserve. Reserve fat in Dutch oven.

Mix flour, salt, pepper and paprika. Coat rabbit pieces with flour mixture. Heat bacon fat until hot. Cook rabbit over medium heat until brown, about 15 minutes. Add mushrooms, onions, thyme and bay leaf. Pour stout over rabbit and vegetables. Crumble reserved bacon over mixture. Heat to boiling; reduce heat. Cover and simmer until thickest pieces of rabbit are done, about 1 hour.

Remove rabbit and vegetables to warm platter; keep warm. Remove bay leaf. Heat stout mixture to boiling. Mix water and cornstarch; stir into stout mixture. Boil and stir 1 minute. Pour sauce over rabbit and vegetables. Sprinkle with parsley.

6 servings

Rabbit Stewed in Stout and Mashed Potatoes with Cabbage (page 61)

VENISON WITH PLUM SAUCE

Plum Barbecue Sauce (see page 76)
6 venison steaks, 1 inch thick (about 4 ounces each)

Prepare Plum Barbecue Sauce. Set oven control to broil. Place venison steaks in greased broiler pan (without rack); spoon ½ cup of the sauce evenly over venison.

Broil venison with tops about 4 inches from heat until light brown, about 10 minutes. Turn venison; spoon ½ cup of the sauce evenly over venison. Broil until rare to medium-rare doneness, about 5 minutes longer. Heat remaining sauce, and serve with venison.

6 servings

STEAMED CLAMS WITH SAUSAGE

AMEIJOAS NA CATAPLANA IS A CENTURIES-OLD DISH FROM PORTUGAL. THERE ARE, UNDERSTANDABLY, MANY VARIATIONS TO THIS DISH. THE RECIPE HERE IS A SPICY, TOMATO-BASED SOUP FLAVORED WITH GARLIC, PAPRIKA AND RED PEPPER.

2 pounds very small clams, about 1½ inches
1 large onion, thinly sliced
3 cloves garlic, chopped
1 small red or green pepper, cut into 1-inch pieces
½ teaspoon paprika
⅛ teaspoon crushed red pepper
2 tablespoons olive or vegetable oil
½ cup dry white wine
½ cup chopped fully cooked smoked ham
1 package (5 ounces) unsliced pepperoni, chopped
1 can (16 ounces) whole tomatoes (with liquid)
2 bay leaves

Clean clams.

Cook and stir onion, garlic, pepper, paprika and crushed red pepper in oil in Dutch oven over medium heat until onion is tender. Stir in remaining ingredients; break up tomatoes with fork. Heat to boiling; reduce heat.

Simmer uncovered 15 minutes. Add clams to vegetable mixture. Cover and simmer 20 minutes. (Do not lift cover or stir.) Remove bay leaves and any unopened clams. Serve with French bread if desired.

4 servings

Steamed Clams with Sausage and Portuguese Sweet Bread (page 134)

SOUTHWEST SAUTÉED SCALLOPS

2 cups water
1 dried Anaheim chile
¼ cup sliced green onions (with tops)
2 tablespoons margarine or butter
2 tablespoons lime juice
2 pounds sea scallops
2 cups cubed fresh pineapple
1 cup Chinese pea pod halves (about 3 ounces)
3 cups hot cooked fettuccine

Heat water to boiling in 1-quart saucepan. Add chile. Boil 5 minutes; drain. Remove stem and seeds; finely chop chile.

Cook and stir onions, margarine, lime juice and chile in 10-inch skillet until margarine is melted. Carefully stir in scallops. Cook over medium heat, stirring frequently, until scallops turn white, about 12 minutes. Stir in the pineapple and pea pods; heat until hot. Remove scallop mixture with slotted spoon; keep warm.

Heat liquid in skillet to boiling. Boil until slightly thickened and reduced by half. Spoon scallop mixture onto fettuccine; pour liquid over scallop mixture.

6 servings

Stir-fried Scallops and Pea Pods

1 pound scallops
1 tablespoon packed brown sugar
1 tablespoon soy sauce
2 teaspoons cornstarch
6 slices bacon, cut into 1-inch pieces
6 green onions (with tops), cut into 1-inch pieces
1 can (8 ounces) sliced water chestnuts, drained
4 ounces fresh Chinese pea pods or 1 package (6 ounces) frozen Chinese pea pods, thawed

If scallops are large, cut into halves. Toss scallops, brown sugar, soy sauce and cornstarch in bowl; cover and refrigerate 10 minutes.

Cook and stir bacon in 10-inch skillet or wok over medium heat until crisp. Drain, reserving 1 tablespoon fat in skillet; reserve bacon.

Cook and stir scallops, onions and water chestnuts in bacon fat over medium-high heat until scallops are white, about 7 minutes; stir in pea pods. Stir in bacon just before serving.

4 servings

Marinated Butterflied Shrimp

1 pound fresh large uncooked shrimp (18 to 20) in shells
½ cup Johannisberg Riesling or dry white wine
1 tablespoon snipped parsley
1 tablespoon vegetable oil
1 tablespoon snipped fresh basil or 1 teaspoon dried basil leaves
¼ teaspoon salt
1 bay leaf, crushed
½ lemon, thinly sliced

Peel shrimp. Make a deep cut lengthwise down back of each shrimp; wash out vein. Press each shrimp flat into butterfly shape. Place shrimp in shallow glass dish or plastic bag. Mix remaining ingredients except lemon slices; pour over shrimp. Cover tightly and refrigerate at least 1 hour.

Arrange shrimp in lightly greased hinged wire grill basket; reserve wine mixture. Cover and grill about 4 inches from medium coals, turning basket and brushing shrimp 2 or 3 times with wine mixture until shrimp are pink, 6 to 10 minutes. Garnish with lemon slices and, if desired, parsley.

4 servings

Broiled Marinated Butterflied Shrimp: Prepare as directed above, except set oven control to broil. Arrange shrimp on lightly greased rack in broiler pan; reserve wine mixture. Broil with tops about 4 inches from heat, turning and brushing once with wine mixture, until shrimp are pink, about 4 minutes each side.

Marinated Butterflied Shrimp

Seafood Chilaquiles Casserole

½ cup vegetable oil
10 flour or corn tortillas (6 to 7 inches in diameter), cut into ½-inch strips
½ cup sliced green onions (with tops)
¼ cup margarine or butter
¼ cup all-purpose flour
½ teaspoon salt
¼ teaspoon pepper
2 cups half-and-half
1 canned chipotle chile in adobo sauce, finely chopped
1 pound bay scallops
1 pound shelled medium raw shrimp
4 slices bacon, crisply cooked and crumbled

Heat oil in 10-inch skillet until hot. Cook tortilla strips in oil until light golden brown, 30 to 60 seconds; drain and reserve.

Cook onions in margarine in 3-quart saucepan over low heat until tender; stir in flour, salt and pepper. Cook, stirring constantly, until mixture is bubbly. Remove from heat; stir in half-and-half. Heat to boiling, stirring constantly. Boil and stir 1 minute; reduce heat. Stir in remaining ingredients except bacon. Cook over medium heat, stirring frequently, just until shrimp are pink, about 9 minutes.

Heat oven to 350°. Layer half of the tortilla strips in bottom of greased 3-quart casserole; top with half of the seafood mixture. Repeat with remaining tortilla strips and seafood mixture; top with bacon. Bake until hot, 15 to 20 minutes.

6 servings

Trout with Cabbage and Apples

Caraway is a spice that enjoys wide popularity, flavoring everything from cheeses, sausages and breads to liquors and liqueurs. Sauerkraut and other traditional German cabbage dishes rarely lack caraway.

5 cups coarsely shredded cabbage (about ½ large head)
¾ cup gewürztraminer or dry white wine
¼ teaspoon salt
¼ teaspoon caraway seed
2 green onions (with tops), thinly sliced
2 medium unpared tart cooking apples, coarsely chopped
4 pan-dressed rainbow trout or whitefish (8 to 10 ounces each)
Vegetable oil

Heat oven to 400°. Heat cabbage, wine, salt, caraway seed and green onions to boiling in 3-quart saucepan; reduce heat. Simmer uncovered, stirring frequently, just until cabbage is limp, about 1 minute. Stir in apples.

Place in ungreased rectangular baking dish, 13 x 9 x 2 inches. Arrange fish on top; brush fish with oil. Bake uncovered until fish flakes easily with fork, about 25 minutes. Garnish with apple slices if desired.

4 servings

Trout with Cabbage and Apples

BLACK SEA BASS WITH FENNEL

FRESH FENNEL ADDS A GENTLE ANISE FLAVOR WHILE THE BASS POACHES IN A BROTH OF DRY WHITE WINE AND LEMON JUICE. SERVE WITH LINGUINE OR OTHER PASTA TOSSED WITH PARMESAN CHEESE AND FRESHLY SNIPPED PARSLEY.

2 large fennel bulbs with green tops
1/4 cup olive or vegetable oil
1 tablespoon lemon juice
1/4 teaspoon salt
Dash of pepper
2 whole black sea bass (about 1 1/2 pounds each), cleaned and scaled
Salt
Pepper
1 cup dry white wine

Cut green tops off fennel bulbs; reserve. Cut bulbs into 1/2-inch slices. Cook and stir fennel slices in oil in 10-inch skillet over medium heat until almost tender, 5 to 7 minutes. Arrange in ungreased rectangular baking dish, 13 x 9 x 2 inches. Sprinkle with lemon juice, 1/4 teaspoon salt and dash of pepper.

Sprinkle cavities of fish with salt and pepper. Arrange some of the reserved fennel greens in fish cavities. Place fish on fennel slices; pour wine over fish. Cook uncovered in 350° oven, spooning juices over fish occasionally, until fish flakes easily with fork, 25 to 30 minutes.

Carefully remove fish to serving platter. Remove fennel slices with slotted spoon; arrange around fish. Garnish with lemon wedges and reserved fennel greens if desired.

4 servings

Grilled Red Snapper with Vegetable Sauté

GRILLED RED SNAPPER WITH VEGETABLE SAUTÉ

Southwest Vegetable Sauté (see page 63)
8 red snapper or cod fillets (about 5 ounces each)
1/4 cup vegetable oil
Salt and pepper

Prepare Southwest Vegetable Sauté and Lime Butter Sauce; keep warm. Generously brush fish fillets with oil; sprinkle with salt and pepper.

Grill over medium coals until fish flakes easily with fork, 10 to 12 minutes. Serve with Southwest Vegetable Sauté and Lime Butter Sauce.

8 servings

BROILED RED SNAPPER: Set oven control to broil. Place fish on rack in broiler pan. Broil with tops about 4 inches from heat until fish flakes easily with fork, 10 to 12 minutes.

PAELLA-STUFFED SNAPPER

A WHOLE STUFFED FISH MAKES A STUNNING PRESENTATION, AND THIS ONE FEEDS A CROWD. PAELLA IS A SPANISH INVENTION THAT COMBINES SEAFOOD AND MEATS WITH SAFFRON-SCENTED RICE. SERRANO CHILES GIVE THE PAELLA STUFFING A MEXICAN KICK.

Paella Stuffing (right)
6- to 8-pound red snapper, cod or lake trout, cleaned and dressed
Lime juice
¼ cup margarine or butter, melted
2 tablespoons lime juice
Lime wedges

Prepare Paella Stuffing. Heat oven to 350°. Rub cavity of fish with lime juice; fill with Paella Stuffing. Close opening with skewers; lace with string. Place in large ungreased broiler pan (without rack) or in shallow roasting pan.

Mix margarine and 2 tablespoons lime juice. Bake fish uncovered, brushing with margarine mixture occasionally, until fish flakes easily with fork, about 1½ hours. Serve with lime wedges.

10 servings

PAELLA STUFFING

½ pound chorizo sausage links, chopped
1 large onion, chopped (about 1 cup)
2 cloves garlic, finely chopped
2 serrano chiles, seeded and chopped
2 tablespoons margarine or butter
2 cups cooked rice
½ cup slivered almonds, toasted (see To Toast, page 25)
¼ cup snipped fresh cilantro (see page 7)
¼ cup tomato sauce
¼ teaspoon ground saffron
1 package (6 ounces) frozen cooked medium shrimp

Cook sausage, onion, garlic and chiles in margarine in 10-inch skillet over medium heat, stirring frequently, until sausage is done, about 10 minutes; drain. Stir in remaining ingredients.

Baked Citrus Swordfish

Citrus Barbecue Sauce (below)
6 swordfish or salmon steaks, 1 inch thick (about 5 ounces each)

Prepare Citrus Barbecue Sauce. Heat oven to 450°. Place swordfish steaks in ungreased rectangular baking dish, 13 x 9 x 2 inches. Pour 1 cup of the sauce over fish.

Bake uncovered until fish flakes easily with fork, 20 to 25 minutes. Serve with remaining Citrus Barbecue Sauce.

6 servings

Citrus Barbecue Sauce

This sauce is the perfect basting mixture for any type of grilled fish.

1 large onion, finely chopped (about 1 cup)
1 tablespoon ground red chiles
¼ teaspoon ground red pepper
1 ancho chile, seeded and finely chopped
1 tablespoon vegetable oil
1 cup orange juice
½ cup lime juice
2 tablespoons sugar
2 tablespoons lemon juice
1 tablespoon snipped fresh cilantro (see page 7)
1 teaspoon salt

Cook onion, ground red chiles, red pepper and ancho chile in oil, stirring frequently, until onion is tender, about 5 minutes. Stir in remaining ingredients.

Heat to boiling; reduce heat to low. Simmer uncovered 10 minutes, stirring occasionally.

Lemon-baked Cod

Fresh codfish and lemon go hand in hand. Serve this simple Norwegian dish with crusty warm bread or piping hot baked potatoes.

1 pound cod fillets
¼ cup margarine or butter, melted
2 tablespoons lemon juice
¼ cup all-purpose flour
½ teaspoon salt
⅛ teaspoon white pepper
Paprika

Heat oven to 350°. If fish fillets are large, cut into serving pieces. Mix margarine and lemon juice. In another bowl, mix flour, salt and white pepper. Dip fish into margarine mixture; coat fish with flour mixture. Place fish in ungreased square baking dish, 8 x 8 x 2 inches. Pour remaining margarine mixture over fish; sprinkle with paprika. Cook uncovered until fish flakes easily with fork, 25 to 30 minutes. Garnish with parsley sprigs and lemon slices if desired.

4 servings

Salmon with Cucumber Salsa

One classic sauce for poached salmon is a creamy one thick with cucumbers. Here, a livelier version benefits from the tang and reduced calories of yogurt.

Cucumber Salsa (right)
2 cups water
1 cup dry white wine
1 teaspoon salt
¼ teaspoon dried thyme leaves
¼ teaspoon dried oregano leaves
⅛ teaspoon ground red pepper
4 black peppercorns
4 cilantro sprigs (see page 7)
1 small onion, sliced
2 pounds salmon fillets, cut into 6 serving pieces

Prepare Cucumber Salsa; reserve. Heat remaining ingredients except fish fillets to boiling in 12-inch skillet; reduce heat. Cover and simmer 5 minutes.

Place fish in skillet; if necessary, add water so that fish is covered. Heat to boiling; reduce heat. Simmer uncovered until fish flakes easily with fork, about 14 minutes.

Carefully remove fish from skillet with slotted spatula; drain on wire rack. Cover and refrigerate until cold, about 2 hours. Serve with Cucumber Salsa.

6 servings

Cucumber Salsa

This recipe makes a good quantity of sauce: three cups. It is extremely versatile. Try it with poached or grilled chicken.

1 cup sour cream
1 cup plain yogurt
¼ cup snipped parsley
¼ cup snipped fresh cilantro (see page 7)
1 teaspoon ground cumin
½ teaspoon salt
2 medium cucumbers, pared, seeded and coarsely shredded

Mix all ingredients. Cover and refrigerate until chilled, about 2 hours.

Salmon with Cucumber Salsa

FISH BAKED IN LETTUCE PACKETS

*6 large or 12 small lettuce leaves**
1 medium carrot, shredded
1 small zucchini, shredded
*1½ pounds fish fillets, cut into 6 serving pieces***
1 tablespoon snipped fresh marjoram leaves or 1 teaspoon dried marjoram leaves
Salt and pepper to taste
Margarine or butter

Heat oven to 400°. Place a few lettuce leaves at a time in hot water. Let stand until wilted, 1 to 2 minutes; drain. Mound a portion of carrot and zucchini near stem end of each lettuce leaf. Place 1 piece fish on vegetables. Sprinkle with marjoram, salt and pepper; dot with margarine.

Fold lettuce leaf over fish; place seam sides down in ungreased rectangular baking dish, 13 x 9 x 2 inches. (Vegetables should be on top of fish.) Cover and bake until fish is done, 25 to 30 minutes.

6 servings

TO MICROWAVE: Prepare lettuce and wrap vegetables and fish as directed above (do not use aluminum foil substitution). Place seam sides down in rectangular microwavable dish, 12 x 7½ x 2 inches. Cover with vented plastic wrap and microwave on high (100%) 4 minutes; rotate dish ½ turn. Microwave until fish is done, 5 to 6 minutes longer.

**6 pieces aluminum foil, about 12 x 8 inches each, can be substituted for the 6 large lettuce leaves. Place 1 piece fish on center of each piece foil; mound a portion of carrot and zucchini on each piece fish. Fold foil over fish and vegetables and seal securely. Place seam side up in baking dish. Do not cover.*

***If using 12 small lettuce leaves, cut fish into 12 pieces.*

Fish Baked in Lettuce Packets

MARINATED BLACK-EYED PEAS

THIS SALAD IS A VARIATION ON THE RUSTIC PORTUGUESE BEAN DISHES POPULAR AROUND LISBON. MARJORAM IS THE EXPECTED HERB, AND WE HAVE ADDED THE FRESH, CITRIC PUNCH OF CILANTRO.

3 cups water
½ pound dried black-eyed peas (about 1½ cups)
1 cup finely chopped onion
¼ cup chopped green pepper
¼ cup olive oil
2 cloves garlic, finely chopped
2 tablespoons snipped fresh cilantro (see page 7)
2 tablespoons red wine vinegar
½ teaspoon salt
½ teaspoon marjoram leaves
¼ teaspoon pepper
3 hard-cooked eggs, sliced

Heat water and peas to boiling in 3-quart saucepan. Boil 2 minutes; reduce heat. Cover and simmer until tender, 50 to 60 minutes; drain. Mix peas and remaining ingredients except 1 hard-cooked egg in large bowl. Cover and refrigerate 3 hours.

Arrange remaining egg on top of mixture; sprinkle with additional snipped cilantro if desired.

5 servings

Pepita Vegetable Burritos

Burritos ("little burros") are a common use of flour tortillas. Here the bundles are stuffed with garlicky, crisp-tender vegetables: broccoli, summer squash and sweet red bell pepper, and served with a rich pumpkin seed sauce.

Pumpkin Seed Sauce (see page 41)
1 cup chopped broccoli
1 medium onion, finely chopped (about ½ cup)
2 cloves garlic, finely chopped
2 tablespoons vegetable oil
1 cup 2 x ¼-inch strips yellow squash
1 cup 2 x ¼-inch strips zucchini
½ cup finely chopped red bell pepper
¼ cup shelled pumpkin seeds, toasted (see To Toast, page 25)
1 tablespoon lemon juice
1 teaspoon ground red chiles
¼ teaspoon salt
¼ teaspoon ground cumin
6 flour tortillas (10 inches in diameter), warmed

Prepare Pumpkin Seed Sauce; reserve. Cook broccoli, onion and garlic in oil in 10-inch skillet, stirring frequently, until tender. Stir in remaining ingredients except tortillas. Cook, stirring occasionally, until squash is crisp-tender, about 2 minutes; keep warm.

Spoon about ½ cup of the vegetable mixture onto center of each tortilla. Fold one end of tortilla up about 1 inch over mixture; fold right and left sides over folded end, overlapping. Fold remaining end down. Serve with Pumpkin Seed Sauce.

6 servings

African Vegetable Stew

Rice simmers along with the vegetables and broth in this South African stew. A dollop of yogurt is a nice counterpoint to the richly seasoned broth.

1 cup chopped onion
½ cup snipped parsley
2 cloves garlic, finely chopped
1 teaspoon ground cinnamon
½ teaspoon ground turmeric
½ teaspoon pepper
¼ teaspoon ground ginger
2 tablespoons margarine or butter
5 cups water
1 cup sliced carrots
½ cup dried lentils
1 cup uncooked regular rice
1 can (16 ounces) whole tomatoes (with liquid)
¾ teaspoon salt
1 package (10 ounces) frozen green peas
1 package (9 ounces) frozen sliced green beans
3 sprigs fresh mint, snipped
Plain yogurt

Cook and stir onion, parsley, garlic, cinnamon, turmeric, pepper and ginger in margarine in Dutch oven until onion is tender. Stir in water, carrots and lentils. Heat to boiling; reduce heat. Cover and cook 25 minutes.

Add rice, tomatoes and salt. Heat to boiling; reduce heat. Cover and cook 20 minutes. Stir in peas, green beans and mint. Heat to boiling; reduce heat. Cover and cook until peas and beans are tender, about 5 minutes. Serve with yogurt.

6 to 8 servings

African Vegetable Stew and Marinated Black-eyed Peas (page 117)
Following pages: Pepita Vegetable Burritos

ZUNI VEGETABLE STEW

THE ZUNI, A TRIBE OF PUEBLO INDIANS, LIVE IN NEW MEXICO. THE FRESH INGREDIENTS THAT MAKE UP THIS HEARTY STEW (VARIOUS CHILES AND SQUASHES, CORN AND BEANS) ARE REPRESENTATIVE OF THAT REGION'S NATIVE BOUNTY.

3/4 cup chopped onion
1 clove garlic, finely chopped
2 tablespoons vegetable oil
1 large red bell pepper, cut into 2 x 1/2-inch strips
2 medium poblano or Anaheim chiles, seeded and cut into 2 x 1/2-inch strips
1 jalapeño chile, seeded and chopped
1 cup cubed Hubbard or acorn squash (about 1/2 pound)
2 cans (14 1/2 ounces each) chicken broth
1/2 teaspoon salt
1/2 teaspoon pepper
1/2 teaspoon ground coriander
1 cup thinly sliced zucchini
1 cup thinly sliced yellow squash
1 can (17 ounces) whole kernel corn, drained
1 can (16 ounces) pinto beans, drained

Cook and stir onion and garlic in oil in Dutch oven over medium heat until onion is tender. Stir in bell pepper, poblano and jalapeño chiles. Cook 15 minutes.

Stir in Hubbard squash, broth, salt, pepper and coriander. Heat to boiling; reduce heat. Cover and simmer until squash is tender, about 15 minutes. Stir in remaining ingredients. Cook uncovered, stirring occasionally, until zucchini is tender, about 10 minutes.

6 servings (about 1 1/3 cups each)

MALAYSIAN OMELET

IN MALAYSIA THIS OMELET IS HARDLY A FORMAL DISH AND IS SOMETIMES OFFERED AS A SNACK. PEANUT OIL WILL NOT BROWN EXCESSIVELY AS BUTTER OR MARGARINE OFTEN DOES WITH LONG COOKING. SERVE THIS THIN OMELET IN WEDGES, AS MALAYSIANS DO.

2 cups thinly sliced eggplant, green pepper and onion
1 tablespoon peanut oil
1 medium onion, finely chopped
1 green chile, seeded and finely chopped (about 1 tablespoon)
1 red chile, seeded and finely chopped (about 1 tablespoon)
1 clove garlic, finely chopped
2 tablespoons peanut oil
4 eggs, beaten
1/4 teaspoon salt
1/4 teaspoon pepper

Cook 2 cups vegetables in 1 tablespoon oil until tender; reserve.

Cook chopped onion, chiles and garlic in 2 tablespoons oil in 10-inch skillet until tender. Mix eggs, salt and pepper; pour into skillet. Cover and cook over low heat until eggs are set and light brown on bottom, about 8 minutes. Cut eggs into wedges; spoon reserved vegetable mixture over omelet.

4 servings

Zuni Vegetable Stew

BLUE CHEESE OMELET WITH PEARS

THE SWEETNESS OF PEARS STRIKES A PERFECT BALANCE WITH THE SHARPNESS OF BLUE CHEESE.

4 eggs
1 tablespoon margarine or butter
¼ cup crumbled Danish blue cheese or Gorgonzola cheese
1 tablespoon snipped chives
1 unpared pear, cut into wedges

Mix eggs with fork just until whites and yolks are blended. Heat margarine in 8-inch skillet or omelet pan over medium-high heat just until margarine begins to brown. As margarine melts, tilt skillet to coat bottom completely.

Quickly pour eggs, all at once, into skillet. Slide skillet back and forth rapidly over heat and, at the same time, stir quickly with fork to spread eggs continuously over bottom of pan as they thicken. Let stand over heat a few seconds to lightly brown bottom of omelet. (Do not overcook—omelet will continue to cook after folding.)

Tilt skillet; run fork under edge of omelet, then jerk skillet sharply to loosen eggs from bottom of skillet. Sprinkle with blue cheese and chives. Fold portion of omelet nearest you just to center. (Allow for portion of omelet to slide up side of skillet.)

Grasp skillet handle; turn omelet onto warm plate, flipping folded portion of omelet over so far side is on bottom. Serve with pear wedges.

2 servings

Blue Cheese Omelet with Pears

BAKED VEGETABLE OMELET

THIS OVEN-BAKED OMELET SERVES SIX, SIMPLIFYING BREAKFAST LOGISTICS AND SATISFYING GUESTS.

1 cup shredded pepper Jack cheese (4 ounces)
1½ cups chopped broccoli or 1 package (10 ounces) frozen chopped broccoli, thawed and drained
2 medium tomatoes, coarsely chopped
2 cups shredded Cheddar cheese (8 ounces)
1 cup milk
¼ cup all-purpose flour
½ teaspoon salt
3 eggs

Heat oven to 350°. Layer pepper cheese, broccoli, tomatoes and Cheddar cheese in ungreased square baking dish, 8 x 8 x 2 inches. Beat milk, flour, salt and eggs until smooth; pour over cheese.

Bake uncovered until egg mixture is set, 40 to 45 minutes. Let stand 10 minutes before cutting.

6 servings

CRABMEAT FRITTATA

4 ounces mushrooms, sliced, or 1 jar (4 ounces) sliced mushrooms, drained
1 bunch green onions (with tops), sliced
¼ cup margarine or butter
1 package (6 ounces) frozen crabmeat, thawed and drained
8 eggs
½ teaspoon lemon and pepper seasoning salt
1 cup shredded Fontina or Monterey Jack cheese (4 ounces)
1 tablespoon snipped fresh basil or 1 teaspoon dried basil leaves
2 tablespoons grated Parmesan cheese

Cook mushrooms and onions in margarine in 10-inch ovenproof skillet, stirring frequently, until tender, about 10 minutes. Stir in crabmeat.

Beat eggs and seasoning salt until blended; stir in Fontina cheese and basil. Pour over crabmeat mixture. Cover and cook over medium-low heat until eggs are set and light brown on bottom, 8 to 10 minutes.

Set oven control to broil. Broil frittata with top about 5 inches from heat until golden brown, about 2 minutes. Sprinkle with Parmesan cheese; cut into wedges.

6 servings

BROCCOLI AND SWISS CHEESE FRITTATA

1 medium onion, chopped
2 cloves garlic, finely chopped
2 tablespoons margarine or butter
1 tablespoon olive or vegetable oil
1 package (10 ounces) frozen chopped broccoli, thawed and drained
8 eggs
½ teaspoon salt
¼ teaspoon pepper
1 cup shredded Swiss cheese
1 to 2 tablespoons snipped fresh oregano or 1 teaspoon dried oregano leaves
2 tablespoons shredded Swiss cheese

Cook onion and garlic in margarine and oil in 10-inch ovenproof skillet over medium heat, stirring frequently, until onion is tender, about 5 minutes. Remove from heat; stir in broccoli.

Beat eggs, salt and pepper until blended; stir in 1 cup cheese and the oregano. Pour over broccoli mixture. Cover and cook over medium-low heat until eggs are set around edge and light brown on bottom, 9 to 11 minutes.

Set oven control to broil. Broil frittata with top about 5 inches from heat until golden brown, about 2 minutes. Sprinkle with 2 tablespoons cheese; cut into wedges.

6 servings

BLUE CHEESE SOUFFLÉ

BLUE CHEESES VARY TREMENDOUSLY IN CHARACTER. TRY A DANISH-STYLE BLUE FOR MELLOW FLAVOR, FRENCH ROQUEFORT FOR SUBTLETY, OR A TRUE FRENCH BLEU FOR MOUTHWATERING SHARPNESS.

2 tablespoons dry bread crumbs
1/4 cup margarine or butter
1/4 cup all-purpose flour
1/8 teaspoon pepper
1/2 cup milk
1/2 cup chardonnay or dry white wine
1/2 package (4-ounce size) blue cheese, crumbled (about 1/2 cup)
3 eggs, separated
1/4 teaspoon cream of tartar
1/2 cup sour cream
1/4 cup whipping cream

Heat oven to 350°. Butter 1-quart soufflé dish or casserole. Make a 4-inch-wide band of triple-thickness aluminum foil 2 inches longer than circumference of dish; butter 1 side of foil. Secure foil band, buttered side in, around outside edge of dish and sprinkle evenly with bread crumbs.

Heat margarine in 2-quart saucepan over low heat until melted. Stir in flour and pepper. Cook over low heat, stirring constantly, until smooth and bubbly; remove from heat. Stir in milk until blended; stir in wine. Heat to boiling, stirring constantly. Boil and stir 1 minute. Stir in cheese until melted; remove from heat.

Beat egg whites and cream of tartar in medium bowl on high speed until stiff but not dry. Beat egg yolks in small bowl on high speed until very thick and lemon colored, about 3 minutes; stir into cheese mixture. Stir about one-fourth of the beaten egg whites into cheese mixture. Fold cheese mixture into remaining egg whites.

Carefully pour into soufflé dish. Bake uncovered until knife inserted halfway between center and edge comes out clean, 50 to 60 minutes. Mix sour cream and whipping cream. Carefully remove foil band, and divide soufflé into portions, using 2 forks. Serve immediately with sour cream mixture. Sprinkle with chopped tomato and avocado, or chopped apples and toasted almonds if desired.

3 servings

Home-style Scrambled Eggs

4 eggs
3 tablespoons water
¾ teaspoon salt
¼ cup margarine or butter
1 cup cubed cooked potato (1 medium)
3 tablespoons finely chopped onion
1 small zucchini, chopped
1 tomato, chopped

Beat eggs, water and salt with fork. Heat margarine in 10-inch skillet over medium heat until melted; cook and stir vegetables in margarine 2 minutes. Pour egg mixture into skillet.

As mixture begins to set at bottom and side, gently lift cooked portions with spatula so that thin, uncooked portion can flow to bottom. Avoid constant stirring. Cook until eggs are thickened throughout but still moist, 3 to 5 minutes.

4 servings

To Microwave: Omit margarine. Beat eggs, water and salt with fork in 1½-quart microwavable casserole. Stir in potato, onion and zucchini. Cover tightly and microwave on high (100%), stirring every minute, until eggs are puffy and set but still moist, 4 to 5 minutes. (Eggs will continue to cook while standing.) Stir in tomato.

Nacho Cheese Puff

1 can (11 ounces) condensed nacho cheese soup
6 eggs, separated
¼ teaspoon cream of tartar

Heat oven to 350°. Butter 2-quart casserole or soufflé dish. Heat soup to boiling over medium heat, stirring constantly; remove from heat. Beat egg whites and cream of tartar in large bowl until stiff but not dry. Beat egg yolks slightly; stir into soup.

Stir about ¼ of the egg white mixture into soup mixture. Fold soup mixture into remaining egg white mixture. Carefully pour into casserole. Bake uncovered until knife inserted halfway between center and edge comes out clean, 50 to 60 minutes. Serve immediately.

6 servings

Individual Nacho Cheese Puffs: Butter six 10-ounce custard cups. Divide mixture evenly among cups; place cups on cookie sheet. Bake 25 to 30 minutes.

Nacho Cheese Puff

Breads, Biscuits and Beyond

Is there anything that speaks of home like the taste and aroma of just-baked bread? That yeasty freshness is really worth waiting for. But you'll be happy to know there are wonderful ways with quick breads, too—muffins to make in minutes, scones, crumpets and mouthwatering pancakes.

Turkish Bread Rings

LIKE CERTAIN MEXICAN BREADS, THESE SESAME RINGS CAN BE BOUGHT ON THE STREET IN TURKEY, WHERE THEY ARE DISPLAYED ON STICKS. SESAME SEEDS GIVE THE RINGS A SUBTLE CRUNCH AND RICH FLAVOR.

2 packages active dry yeast
1½ cups warm water (105 to 115°)
1½ cups lukewarm milk (scalded, then cooled)
2 tablespoons sugar
1 tablespoon salt
2 tablespoons vegetable oil
6½ to 7 cups all-purpose flour
1 egg
2 teaspoons water
¾ cup sesame seed

Dissolve yeast in warm water in large bowl. Stir in milk, sugar, salt, oil and 3 cups of the flour. Beat until smooth. Stir in enough remaining flour to make dough easy to handle. Turn dough onto generously floured surface; knead until smooth and elastic, about 5 minutes. Place in greased bowl; turn greased side up. Cover; let rise in warm place until double, about 45 minutes. (Dough is ready if indentation remains when touched.)

Punch down dough; divide into 8 equal parts. Roll and shape each part into a rope about 24 inches long; moisten ends with water. Bring ends of rope together, and pinch to form a ring about 6 inches in diameter. Beat egg and 2 teaspoons water with fork. Spread sesame seed on dinner plate. Brush each ring with egg mixture; dip into sesame seed. Place rings, sesame seed side up, on large greased cookie sheets. Cover loosely; let rise until double, about 30 minutes.

Heat oven to 400°. Bake until rings are golden brown, 18 to 20 minutes.

8 bread rings

Clockwise from top: Turkish Bread Rings, Yugoslavian Coffee Cake (page 132) and Coconut Corn Bread (page 143)

Yugoslavian Coffee Cake

Walnut-filllled dough is wound into a snail shape. Slices of this sweet coffee cake are spectacularly traced with the filling.

1 package active dry yeast
¼ cup warm water (105 to 115°)
¾ cup lukewarm milk (scalded, then cooled)
½ cup margarine or butter, softened
3 eggs
¼ cup sugar
½ teaspoon salt
4½ to 5 cups all-purpose flour
Walnut Filling (right)
Glaze (right)

Dissolve yeast in warm water in large bowl. Stir in milk, margarine, eggs, sugar, salt and 3 cups of the flour. Beat until smooth. Stir in enough remaining flour to make dough easy to handle.

Turn dough onto lightly floured surface; knead until smooth and elastic, about 5 minutes. Place in greased bowl; turn greased side up. Cover; let rise in warm place until double, 1 to 1½ hours. (Dough is ready if indentation remains when touched.) While dough is rising, make Walnut Filling and Glaze.

Punch down dough; divide into halves. Roll each half into rectangle, 15 x 12 inches, on lightly floured surface. Spread half the Walnut Filling over each rectangle. Roll up tightly, beginning at 15-inch side. Pinch edge of dough into each roll to seal well. Stretch rolls to make even. With sealed edges down, coil into snail shapes on lightly greased cookie sheets. Cover; let rise until double, about 1 hour. Heat oven to 350°. Bake until golden brown, 35 to 45 minutes. Brush with margarine if desired; spread with Glaze.

2 coffee cakes

Walnut Filling

2½ cups finely chopped walnuts
1 cup packed brown sugar
⅓ cup margarine or butter, softened
1 egg
2 teaspoons ground cinnamon

Mix all ingredients.

Glaze

1 cup powdered sugar
1 to 2 tablespoons water

Mix all ingredients until smooth and of desired consistency.

Italian Focaccia

Focaccia is as flavorful as a simple country bread can get. Olive oil and fresh rosemary give this yeast-raised flatbread its glorious Italian flavor.

1 package active dry yeast
1 cup warm water (105 to 115°)
2 to 3 tablespoons snipped fresh rosemary
3 tablespoons olive oil
2 teaspoons salt
2½ to 3 cups all-purpose flour
Olive oil
Coarsely ground pepper (optional)
Olive oil

Dissolve yeast in warm water in large bowl. Stir in rosemary, 3 tablespoons oil, the salt and enough flour to make dough easy to handle. Turn dough onto lightly floured surface; knead until smooth and elastic, 5 to 10 minutes. Place in greased bowl; turn greased side up. Cover; let rise in warm place until double, about 1 hour. (Dough is ready if indentation remains when touched.)

Heat oven to 400°. Punch down dough. Press in oiled 12-inch pizza pan. Make depressions, with fingers about 2 inches apart, on top of dough. Brush with oil; sprinkle with pepper. Let rise uncovered 30 minutes. Bake until golden brown, 20 to 25 minutes. Brush with additional oil. Serve warm.

1 focaccia

BRAN-SUNFLOWER NUT BREAD

SATISFACTION ON A SATURDAY MORNING CAN COME WITH THE IRRESISTIBLE AROMA OF WHOLESOME, HOMEMADE BREAD.

5½ to 6 cups all-purpose flour
1½ cups shreds of bran cereal
2 tablespoons sugar
2 teaspoons salt
2 packages active dry yeast
1½ cups water
1 cup milk
¼ cup dark molasses
¼ cup margarine or butter
1 cup sunflower nuts
Margarine or butter, softened

Mix 2 cups of the flour, the cereal, sugar, salt and yeast in a large bowl. Heat water, milk, molasses and ¼ cup margarine to 125 to 130° (margarine may not melt completely); stir into flour mixture. Beat on low speed 1 minute, scraping bowl frequently. Beat on medium speed 1 minute, scraping bowl frequently. Stir in sunflower nuts and enough remaining flour, 1 cup at a time, to make dough easy to handle; turn onto lightly floured surface.

Knead until elastic, about 5 minutes. Place in greased bowl; turn greased side up. Cover and let rise in warm place until double, about one hour. (Dough is ready if indentation remains when touched.)

Grease 2 loaf pans, 8½ x 4½ x 2½ inches. Punch down dough; divide into halves. Flatten each into oblong, pressing out air. Fold lengthwise into halves; flatten again. Lift at each end and pull, slapping on work surface several times, until 15 x 5 inches. Fold crosswise into thirds, overlapping; press down firmly to seal. Roll dough tightly toward you, beginning at one open end and pressing after each turn to seal. Roll back and forth to tighten; press each end with side of hand to seal. Place seam side down in pans. Brush with margarine. Let rise until double, 40 to 60 minutes.

Heat oven to 375°. Place loaves on low rack so that tops of pans are in center of oven. Pans should not touch each other or sides of oven. Bake until deep golden brown and loaves sound hollow when tapped, 30 to 35 minutes. Remove from pans. Brush with margarine; cool on wire rack.

2 loaves

Note: To make round loaves, grease large cookie sheet. Punch dough down and divide into halves. Shape each half into round, slightly flattened loaf. Place loaves in opposite corners of cookie sheet and let rise and bake as directed.

Casserole Bread

1 package active dry yeast
½ cup warm water (105 to 115°)
½ cup lukewarm milk (scalded, then cooled)
⅔ cup margarine or butter, softened
2 eggs
1 teaspoon salt
3 cups all-purpose flour
Margarine or butter, softened

Dissolve yeast in warm water in large mixer bowl. Add milk, ⅔ cup margarine, the eggs, salt and 1 cup of the flour. Beat on low speed, scraping bowl constantly, 30 seconds. Beat on medium speed, scraping bowl occasionally, 2 minutes. Stir in remaining flour until smooth. Scrape batter from side of bowl. Cover; let rise in warm place until double, about 30 minutes. (Batter is ready if indentation remains when touched with floured finger.)

Stir down batter by beating about 25 strokes. Spread evenly in greased 2-quart casserole. Cover; let rise until double, about 40 minutes.

Heat oven to 375°. Place loaf on low rack so that top of casserole is in center of oven. Casserole should not touch sides of oven. Bake until loaf is brown and sounds hollow when tapped, 40 to 45 minutes. Immediately remove from casserole. Brush top of loaf with margarine; cool on wire rack. To serve, cut into wedges with serrated knife.

1 loaf

Portuguese Sweet Bread

Up and down the Northeastern seaboard of the United States are fans of this melt-in-your-mouth bread. Some say it came to our shores with the influx of Portuguese sailors during the American whaling boom.

2 packages active dry yeast
¼ cup warm water (105 to 115°)
1 cup lukewarm milk (scalded, then cooled)
¾ cup sugar
1 teaspoon salt
3 eggs
½ cup margarine or butter, softened
5½ to 6 cups all-purpose flour
1 egg
1 teaspoon sugar

Dissolve yeast in warm water in large bowl. Stir in milk, ¾ cup sugar, the salt, 3 eggs, the margarine and 3 cups of the flour. Beat until smooth. Stir in enough remaining flour to make dough easy to handle.

Turn dough onto lightly floured surface: knead until smooth and elastic, about 5 minutes. Place in greased bowl; turn greased side up. Cover; let rise in warm place until double, 1½ to 2 hours. (Dough is ready if indentation remains when touched.)

Punch down dough; divide into halves. Shape each half into a round, slightly flat loaf. Place each loaf in greased round layer pan, 9 x 1½ inches. Cover; let rise until double, about 1 hour. Heat oven to 350°. Beat 1 egg slightly; brush over loaves. Sprinkle with 1 teaspoon sugar. Bake until loaves are golden brown, 35 to 45 minutes.

2 loaves

Snail Loaves: After dividing dough into halves, roll each half into a rope about 25 x 1½ inches. Coil each to form a snail shape in greased round layer pan, 9 x 1½ inches. Continue as directed.

Australian Damper Bread

Australian Damper Bread

Damper bread, scarcely more complicated than biscuits, may have been named for one William Dampier, an early explorer of Australia.

1 package active dry yeast
¼ cup warm water (105 to 115°)
2 tablespoons sugar
3 cups all-purpose flour
1 tablespoon baking powder
¾ teaspoon salt
¼ cup shortening
1 cup buttermilk

Dissolve yeast in warm water; stir in sugar. Mix flour, baking powder and salt in large bowl; cut in shortening until mixture resembles fine crumbs. Stir in yeast mixture and buttermilk until soft dough forms. Turn dough onto lightly floured surface; gently knead until smooth, about 1 minute. Cover; let rest 10 minutes. Shape dough into a round loaf, about 7 inches in diameter. Place on greased cookie sheet. Cover; let rise in warm place 30 minutes.

Heat oven to 375°. Cut an X about ½ inch deep in top of bread. Bake until loaf is golden brown, about 35 minutes. Serve warm. Tear bread into pieces to serve.

1 loaf

ADOBE BREAD

ALTHOUGH AUTHENTIC PUEBLO BREAD CAN'T BE EXACTLY DUPLICATED IN ORDINARY OVENS, THE CRUSTY SUBSTITUTE HERE USES WHOLE WHEAT FLOUR, AS THE PUEBLO INDIANS WOULD.

2 cups whole wheat flour
¼ cup sugar
¼ cup shortening or lard
2 teaspoons salt
2 packages active dry yeast
2 cups very warm water (120 to 130°)
3 to 4 cups all-purpose flour
2 teaspoons all-purpose flour

Mix whole wheat flour, sugar, shortening, salt and yeast in large bowl; stir in warm water. Beat on low speed 1 minute, scraping bowl frequently. Beat on medium speed 1 minute, scraping bowl frequently. Stir in enough all-purpose flour, 1 cup at a time, to make dough easy to handle.

Turn dough onto lightly floured surface; knead until smooth and elastic, about 10 minutes. Place in greased medium bowl; turn greased side up. Cover and let rise in warm place until double, 40 to 60 minutes. (Dough is ready if indentation remains when dough is touched.)

Punch down dough; divide into halves. Let rest 5 minutes. Shape each half into a round, slightly flat loaf. Place loaves on opposite corners of greased large cookie sheet. Cover and let rise until double, 40 to 50 minutes.

Heat oven to 375°. Make ½-inch-deep slashes across top of each loaf in lattice design. Sprinkle each loaf with 1 teaspoon all-purpose flour. Bake until loaves are deep golden brown and sound hollow when tapped, 35 to 40 minutes. Cool on wire rack.

2 loaves

Adobe Bread

CRUMPETS

CRUMPETS ARE BRITISH GRIDDLE CAKES. THE BATTER IS POURED INTO METAL RINGS, AND WHEN THE CAKES HAVE "SET" THE RINGS ARE REMOVED SO THAT THE CRUMPETS CAN BE TURNED OVER. CRUMPETS HAVE LARGE HOLES—JUST RIGHT FOR CATCHING LOTS OF MARMALADE OR BUTTER—AND, LIKE MANY FRIED FOODS, ARE MOST DELICIOUS WHEN THEY ARE HOT.

1 package dry active yeast
¼ cup warm water (105 to 115°)
½ cup lukewarm milk (scalded, then cooled)
1 tablespoon margarine or butter
1 teaspoon sugar
¾ teaspoon salt
1 egg
1 cup all-purpose flour

Dissolve yeast in warm water in medium bowl. Stir in remaining ingredients; beat until smooth. Cover; let rise in warm place until double, 40 to 60 minutes.

Grease griddle or heavy skillet and insides of four to six 3-inch flan rings or crumpet rings.* Place rings on griddle over medium heat until hot. Pour about 2 tablespoons batter into each ring. Cook until tops form bubbles and bottoms are golden brown, 1 to 2 minutes. Remove rings; turn crumpets to brown other side, 1 to 2 minutes. Repeat with remaining batter, greasing insides of rings each time. Serve with margarine or butter and jam or marmalade if desired.

12 crumpets

**6½-ounce tuna, minced clam or shrimp cans, tops and bottoms removed, can be substituted for the flan rings.*

Oat-Peach Muffins

Mix these up in minutes to make any morning feel like a weekend.

- *1 cup quick-cooking oats*
- *1 cup buttermilk*
- *¼ cup vegetable oil*
- *2 tablespoons light molasses*
- *1 teaspoon vanilla*
- *1 egg*
- *1¼ cups all-purpose flour*
- *¾ cup ¼-inch pieces fresh peaches, or well-drained canned or frozen and thawed peach slices*
- *¾ cup coarsely chopped walnuts*
- *¼ cup packed brown sugar*
- *1½ teaspoons ground cinnamon*
- *1 teaspoon baking soda*
- *1 teaspoon baking powder*
- *½ teaspoon salt*

Heat oven to 400°. Grease bottoms only of six 6-ounce custard cups, or 10 large muffin cups, 3 x 1¼ inches, or 12 muffin cups, 2½ x 1¼ inches. Mix oats and buttermilk in large bowl; beat in oil, molasses, vanilla and egg with fork. Stir in remaining ingredients just until flour is moistened. Divide batter among cups (cups will be full). If using custard cups, place on cooking sheet.

Bake until wooden pick inserted in center comes out clean, custard cups 20 to 25 minutes, muffin cups 15 to 20 minutes. Immediately remove from cups.

6 jumbo, 10 large or 12 medium muffins

Note: Dates or raisins can be substituted for the peaches.

Blueberry Streusel Muffins

- *Streusel Topping (below)*
- *1 egg*
- *2 cups variety baking mix*
- *⅔ cup milk*
- *3 tablespoons sugar*
- *1 tablespoon vegetable oil*
- *¾ cup fresh or frozen (thawed and drained) blueberries*

Heat oven to 400°. Grease bottoms only of 12 medium muffin cups, 2½ x 1¼ inches, or line with paper baking cups. Prepare Streusel Topping.

Beat egg slightly in medium bowl; stir in remaining ingredients except blueberries and Streusel Topping just until moistened. Fold in blueberries. Divide batter evenly among muffin cups; sprinkle with topping. Bake until golden brown, 18 to 20 minutes.

12 muffins

Streusel Topping

- *3 tablespoons variety baking mix*
- *2 tablespoons packed brown sugar*
- *2 teaspoons firm margarine or butter*

Mix baking mix and packed brown sugar. Cut in margarine or butter until mixture becomes crumbly.

PROSCIUTTO, SUN-DRIED TOMATO AND BASIL MUFFINS

1 egg
1 cup milk
¼ cup vegetable oil
2 cups all-purpose flour
¾ cup finely chopped prosciutto (about ¼ pound)
½ cup chopped sun-dried tomatoes in olive oil, rinsed and drained
2 tablespoons snipped fresh basil leaves
2½ teaspoons baking powder

Heat oven to 400°. Grease four 6-ounce custard cups. Beat egg in large bowl; stir in milk and oil. Stir in remaining ingredients just until flour is moistened.

Divide batter among cups (cups will be full). Place on cookie sheet.

Bake until golden brown, about 35 minutes. Immediately remove from cups.

4 muffins

BACON AND PIMIENTO-BASIL MUFFINS: Substitute ¾ pound bacon, crisply cooked and crumbled, for the prosciutto. Substitute 1 jar (2 ounces) sliced pimientos, drained, for the tomatoes; stir in ½ teaspoon salt with the baking powder.

ITALIAN SAUSAGE MUFFINS: Substitute ⅓ pound bulk Italian sausage, cooked and drained, for the prosciutto. Decrease basil to 1 tablespoon and add 1 tablespoon snipped fresh oregano.

Do-ahead Note: Wrap, label and freeze muffins up to 3 months.

VEGETABLE CORNMEAL MUFFINS

THESE SPICY AND COLORFUL MUFFINS ARE THE PERFECT ADDITION TO A SOUTHWESTERN MEAL.

1¼ cups yellow cornmeal
¾ cup all-purpose flour
¼ cup shortening
1½ cups buttermilk
2 teaspoons baking powder
1 teaspoon sugar
1 teaspoon salt
½ teaspoon baking soda
2 eggs
1 cup shredded zucchini, drained
½ cup chopped red bell pepper
2 tablespoons chopped jalapeño or serrano chiles

Heat oven to 450°. Grease 16 medium muffin cups, 2½ x 1¼ inches, or line muffin cups with paper baking cups.

Mix all ingredients except zucchini, bell pepper and chiles; beat vigorously 30 seconds. Stir in remaining ingredients.

Fill muffin cups about ⅞ full. Bake until light golden brown, 20 to 25 minutes. Remove from pan immediately.

16 muffins

Raisin Scones

For almond-flavored scones, replace raisins with 1/4 teaspoon almond extract and 2 tablespoons coarsely chopped almonds.

2 cups variety baking mix
1/2 cup raisins
1/3 cup whipping cream
3 tablespoons sugar
1 egg
Milk
Sugar

Heat oven to 425°. Grease cookie sheet. Mix baking mix, raisins, whipping cream, 3 tablespoons sugar and the egg until lumpy dough forms.

Pat into 8-inch circle on cookie sheet (if dough is too sticky, dip fingers in baking mix); brush top with milk and sprinkle with sugar. Cut into 8 wedges.

Bake until golden brown, about 12 minutes; separate carefully. Serve warm.

8 scones

Navajo Fry Breads

Navajo Fry Bread is a Santa Fe specialty that has become popular throughout the Southwest. A hole is always poked through the center of each round of dough so that the bread puffs spectacularly when cooked in hot oil.

2 cups all-purpose flour
2 teaspoons baking powder
1 teaspoon salt
2 tablespoons shortening
2/3 cup warm water
Vegetable oil

Mix flour, baking powder and salt; cut in shortening until mixture resembles fine crumbs. Sprinkle in water, 1 tablespoon at a time, tossing with fork until all flour is moistened and dough almost cleans side of bowl. Gather into ball; cover and refrigerate 30 minutes.

Heat oil (1 inch) to 400° in Dutch oven. Divide dough into 12 equal pieces. Roll each piece into 6-inch circle on lightly floured surface. Let rest a few minutes.

Make a hole about 1/2 inch in diameter in center of each circle. Fry circles, turning once, until puffed and golden, about 1 minute on each side; drain. Serve warm.

12 breads

Chutney Quick Bread

Afternoon tea takes on an international flavor with this tasty loaf.

2½ cups all-purpose flour
½ cup granulated sugar
½ cup packed brown sugar
1¼ cups milk
3 tablespoons vegetable oil
1 tablespoon grated orange peel
3½ teaspoons baking powder
1 teaspoon salt
1 egg
1 cup chopped nuts
¾ cup mild chutney
Spreads (right)

Heat oven to 350°. Grease loaf pan, 9 x 5 x 3 inches. Mix flour, sugars, milk, oil, orange peel, baking powder, salt and egg in large bowl. Beat on low speed, scraping bowl constantly, until moistened. Beat on medium speed, scraping bowl occasionally, 30 seconds.

Stir in nuts and chutney. Pour into prepared pan.

Bake until wooden pick inserted in center comes out clean, 60 to 65 minutes. (If bread becomes too dark, cover loosely with aluminum foil last 20 minutes.) Cool slightly; remove from pan. Cool completely on wire rack. Serve with one or more of the spreads.

1 loaf

Curried Spread

1 package (8 ounces) cream cheese, softened
2 teaspoons sugar
2 teaspoons curry powder
Dash of salt

Beat all ingredients until smooth.

Lemon-Cheese Spread

1 package (8 ounces) cream cheese, softened
1 tablespoon powdered sugar
1 teaspoon grated lemon peel
1 tablespoon lemon juice

Beat all ingredients on medium speed until fluffy.

Whipped Honey-Orange Butter

1 cup margarine or butter, softened
2 tablespoons honey
2 teaspoons grated orange peel

Beat all ingredients on medium speed until fluffy.

Chinese Green Onion Circles

Chinese Green Onion Circles

These coiled little pastries taste faintly of sesame oil, but green onions are the dominant flavor.

3 cups all-purpose flour
1½ teaspoons baking powder
1 teaspoon salt
1 tablespoon sesame oil
1 cup plus 1 to 2 tablespoons cold water
Sesame oil
¾ cup chopped green onions
Vegetable oil

Mix flour, baking powder and salt in medium bowl; stir in 1 tablespoon sesame oil and enough water to make a smooth, soft dough. Turn dough onto floured surface; knead 3 minutes. Divide dough into 6 equal parts; keep covered. Roll each part into circle, about 7 inches in diameter. Brush each circle with sesame oil, and sprinkle with about 2 tablespoons of the green onions. Roll each circle up tightly, pinching side and ends to seal. Shape into rope, about 12 inches long. Roll to form a coil, tucking end under coil; flatten into circle, about 7 inches in diameter.

Heat 2 tablespoons vegetable oil in 8-inch skillet until hot. Cook 1 circle over medium heat until golden brown, about 8 minutes on each side. Repeat with additional oil and remaining circles. Cut into wedges; serve hot.

6 circles

COCONUT CORN BREAD

CORNMEAL GIVES THIS TROPICALLY FLAVORED LOAF FROM THE DOMINICAN REPUBLIC CRUNCH. SPICES, FRESH COCONUT, COCONUT CREAM AND RUM FLAVOR THIS SWEET BREAD, WHICH IS STUDDED WITH CANDIED FRUIT.

½ cup diced mixed candied fruit
2 tablespoons dark rum
⅓ cup sugar
⅓ cup margarine or butter, softened
2 eggs
1 cup coconut cream
1 cup yellow cornmeal
1 cup all-purpose flour
1½ teaspoons baking powder
½ teaspoon salt
½ teaspoon ground cinnamon
¼ teaspoon ground cloves
1 cup shredded fresh coconut

Heat oven to 375°. Mix candied fruit and rum in small bowl; reserve. Beat sugar and margarine in large bowl; add eggs, one at a time, beating until well blended. Stir in remaining ingredients except candied fruit mixture and coconut; beat until smooth, about 30 strokes by hand. Fold in candied fruit mixture and coconut. Pour into greased loaf pan, 8½ x 4½ x 2½ inches. Bake until top is golden brown and wooden pick inserted in center comes out clean, 40 to 45 minutes. Cool 20 minutes; remove from pan. Cool completely before slicing.

1 loaf

COCONUT PANCAKES

THE THAIS ARE KNOWN FOR THEIR INVENTIVENESS WITH COCONUT—THE MEAT, THE MILK AND COCONUT CREAM. THESE SWEET PANCAKES, LIGHT WITH RICE FLOUR, ARE OFFERED FRESH AND WARM IN THAI MARKETS. THEY ARE DELICATE, THINNER THAN AMERICAN PANCAKES AND MORE LIKE CRÈPES.

1 cup rice flour
¼ cup sugar
½ teaspoon salt
1 can (14 ounces) unsweetened coconut milk
4 eggs
¾ cup shredded coconut
Vegetable oil
Red and green food colors
Sweetened condensed milk
Shredded coconut

Beat flour, sugar, salt, coconut milk and eggs in medium bowl until smooth. Stir in ¾ cup coconut. Divide batter equally among 3 bowls. Tint one part of batter pale pink with red food color, and one part pale green with green food color; leave third part untinted. Lightly oil 8-inch nonstick skillet; heat until hot. For each pancake, pour scant ¼ cup batter into skillet; immediately rotate skillet until batter covers bottom.

Cook until top is almost dry and bottom is light brown. Run wide spatula around edge to loosen; turn and cook other side until light brown. Roll up pancake, and place on heatproof platter; keep warm. Drizzle with sweetened condensed milk, and sprinkle with coconut.

About 18 pancakes

AFTERTHOUGHTS

There's no such thing as a complete meal without at least a mouthful of sweetness at the end. Whether it's a compote of colorful fruit in season or a smashing do-ahead mousse, here you'll find the finest finales from every corner of the world.

SOUTHWEST LEMON FRUIT TART

A PERFECT CONTRAST TO A SPICY SOUTHWESTERN MEAL, THIS IS A BEAUTIFUL TART, SENSATIONAL WITH ITS GLISTENING ARRANGEMENT OF COLORFUL FRUITS.

Pecan Crust (right)
1 teaspoon unflavored gelatin
1 tablespoon cold water
½ cup sugar
2 eggs
2 tablespoons grated lemon peel
¼ cup lemon juice
½ cup whipping cream
1 cup strawberry halves
1 cup raspberries
½ cup blackberries or blueberries
1 mango or papaya (see page 7), pared and sliced
⅓ cup guava jelly or apricot jam, melted

Southwest Lemon Fruit Tart

Prepare Pecan Crust; cool. Sprinkle gelatin on cold water in 1½-quart saucepan to soften. Beat sugar and eggs until thick and lemon colored; stir into gelatin mixture. Heat just to boiling over low heat, stirring constantly, about 15 minutes. Remove from heat; stir in lemon peel and juice.

Beat whipping cream in chilled medium bowl until soft peaks form. Fold in lemon mixture; pour into Pecan Crust. Refrigerate at least 2 hours. Arrange fruits on top; drizzle with jelly. Refrigerate any remaining tart.

8 servings

PECAN CRUST

1 cup all-purpose flour
½ cup finely chopped pecans
¼ cup sugar
¼ cup margarine or butter, softened
1 egg

Heat oven to 375°. Mix flour, pecans and sugar; mix in margarine and egg until crumbly. Press in bottom and up side of greased tart pan, 9 x 1 inch. Bake until light golden brown, 15 to 20 minutes.

HONEY-WINE CRANBERRY TART

CRANBERRIES AREN'T JUST FOR HOLIDAYS! THIS TART FEATURES CRANBERRIES WITH CRUNCHY WALNUTS AND A HINT OF ORANGE.

Cookie Crust (below)
⅓ cup orange marmalade
½ cup coarsely chopped walnuts
1 envelope unflavored gelatin
¼ cup cold water
1 cup sauvignon blanc or dry white wine
½ cup honey
1 package (12 ounces) fresh cranberries
Sweetened whipped cream

Heat oven to 375°. Prepare Cookie Crust. Press in bottom and 1½ inches up side of ungreased springform pan, 9 x 3 inches. Bake until crust is set and light brown, 18 to 20 minutes. Spread orange marmalade on bottom; sprinkle with nuts.

Sprinkle gelatin on cold water in 3-quart saucepan. Let stand until gelatin is softened, about 5 minutes. Stir in remaining ingredients except whipped cream. Heat to boiling; reduce heat slightly. Boil uncovered 5 minutes. Cool 15 minutes.

Pour cranberry mixture over nuts in crust. Cover and refrigerate until chilled, at least 4 hours. Remove side of pan. Serve with whipped cream.

8 to 10 servings

COOKIE CRUST

1¾ cups all-purpose flour
½ cup powdered sugar
¾ cup margarine or butter, softened

Mix all ingredients until crumbly; mix with hands until dough forms.

BROWN SUGAR PEAR TART

HERE'S A FRESH FRUIT DESSERT YOU CAN MAKE ALL YEAR-ROUND.

Lemony Nut Crust (below)
4 medium pears (about two pounds), pared
½ cup packed brown sugar
2 tablespoons all-purpose flour
½ teaspoon ground cinnamon

Bake Lemony Nut Crust. Cut each pear lengthwise into halves; remove core. Place each pear half, cut side down, on cutting surface. Cut crosswise into thin slices. With spatula, lift each pear half and arrange on crust, fanning and overlapping slices (retain pear shape) to cover surface of crust.

Mix brown sugar, flour and cinnamon; sprinkle over pears. Bake in 375° oven until crust is golden brown and pears are tender, 15 to 20 minutes.

8 servings

LEMONY NUT CRUST

1⅓ cups all-purpose flour
⅓ cup packed brown sugar
⅓ cup finely chopped pecans
½ teaspoon ground nutmeg
½ teaspoon grated lemon peel
⅔ cup margarine or butter, softened

Heat oven to 375°. Mix all ingredients except margarine; cut in margarine until crumbly. Press firmly and evenly against bottom and side of ungreased 12-inch pizza pan. Bake 8 minutes.

Honey-Wine Cranberry Tart

Peach Cobbler with Caramel Sauce

1/4 cup packed brown sugar
1 tablespoon lemon juice
1/2 teaspoon ground cinnamon
3 pounds peaches, sliced, or 2 packages (16 ounces each) frozen sliced peaches, thawed and drained
3/4 cup all-purpose flour
1/2 cup granulated sugar
2 teaspoons baking powder
1/4 teaspoon salt
3/4 cup whipping cream
1/4 cup margarine or butter, melted
Caramel Sauce (below)

Heat oven to 375°. Mix brown sugar, lemon juice, cinnamon and peaches; place in greased shallow 2½-quart casserole. Mix flour, granulated sugar, baking powder and salt; stir in whipping cream and margarine until well blended. Spoon batter evenly over fruit.

Bake until crust is deep golden brown, 40 to 45 minutes. Serve warm with warm Caramel Sauce.

8 servings

Caramel Sauce

1 cup packed brown sugar
1/2 cup whipping cream
1/4 cup corn syrup
1 tablespoon margarine or butter
2 teaspoons ground cinnamon

Heat all ingredients to boiling over medium heat, stirring constantly; reduce heat to low. Simmer uncovered 5 minutes.

Watermelon with Blackberries and Pear Purée

Beautiful and light, this dessert is total satisfaction without guilt.

3 slices watermelon, each 3/4 inch thick
1 1/2 cups blackberries
Pear Purée (below)

Cut each watermelon slice into 10 wedges. Cut rind from wedges; remove seeds. Arrange wedges on 6 dessert plates; top with blackberries. Top each serving with Pear Purée.

6 servings

Pear Purée

2 medium pears, pared
1/4 cup light rum

Cut pears into fourths and remove cores and stems. Place pears and rum in workbowl of food processor fitted with steel blade or in blender container. Cover and process until smooth, about 1 minute.

TROPICAL FRUIT WITH CHOCOLATE SAUCE

ON THE ISLAND OF CURAÇAO, THEY MAKE AND ENJOY A LIGHT-BODIED, ORANGE-FLAVORED LIQUEUR. FRESH FRUIT ALLOWED TO MACERATE (SOAK OR MARINATE) IN SWEET LIQUEUR BECOMES EVEN MORE SUCCULENT. SELECT THE TROPICAL FRUITS YOU LOVE BEST FOR THIS SIMPLE—BUT SOPHISTICATED—DESSERT.

Chocolate Sauce (below)
*3 to 4 cups assorted fresh tropical fruit, cut up**
2 to 3 tablespoons orange-flavored liqueur or rum

Prepare Chocolate Sauce. Toss fruit and liqueur. Cover and refrigerate, stirring once or twice, at least 1 hour. Spoon fruit into dessert dishes; drizzle with Chocolate Sauce.

6 to 8 servings

**Suggested fruits are banana, pineapple, strawberries, papaya, mango and carambola (see page 7).*

CHOCOLATE SAUCE

1 package (6 ounces) semisweet chocolate chips
½ cup evaporated milk
½ cup sugar
2 teaspoons margarine or butter
1 tablespoon orange-flavored liqueur or rum

Heat chocolate, milk and sugar to boiling over medium heat, stirring constantly; remove from heat. Stir in margarine and liqueur. Let stand 1 hour. Cover and refrigerate any remaining sauce.

FRESH FRUIT WITH FRENCH CREAM

FRENCH CRÈME FRAÎCHE IS SOMETHING LIKE SOUR CREAM BUT LESS ACID OR "SOURED" TASTING. THE SAUCE BELOW IS OUR QUICK VERSION.

⅔ cup whipping cream
⅓ cup sour cream
*2 to 3 cups assorted fresh fruit**
Ground nutmeg or sugar

Gradually stir whipping cream into sour cream. Cover and refrigerate no longer than 48 hours. Serve over fruit. Sprinkle with nutmeg.

4 to 6 servings

**Suggested fruits are blueberries, raspberries, strawberries, sliced peaches or cubed pineapple.*

FOLLOWING PAGES: Fresh Fruit with French Cream and Tropical Fruit with Chocolate Sauce

Diving
Brand
California APPLES

PUFFY APPLE OMELET

2 tablespoons margarine or butter
2 medium unpared tart apples, cut into ½-inch slices
¼ cup French colombard or dry white wine
6 eggs, separated
¼ cup French colombard or dry white wine
½ teaspoon salt
¼ cup sliced green onions (with tops)

Heat oven to 325°. Heat margarine in 10-inch ovenproof skillet over medium heat until melted. Stir in apple slices and ¼ cup wine. Cook uncovered over medium heat, stirring occasionally, just until liquid has evaporated, about 10 minutes.

While apples cook, beat egg whites, ¼ cup wine and the salt in large bowl on high speed until stiff but not dry. Beat egg yolks in medium bowl on high speed until very thick and lemon colored, about 3 minutes. Fold beaten egg yolks and green onions into egg whites.

Pour egg mixture over apple mixture in skillet; level surface gently. Cook uncovered over low heat until puffy and light brown on edge. About 5 minutes. (Lift omelet carefully at edge to judge color.)

Carefully place skillet in oven. Bake uncovered until knife inserted in center comes out clean, about 12 minutes. Invert on heatproof serving plate if desired. Cut into wedges.

4 servings

Puffy Apple Omelet

THE ULTIMATE CHOCOLATE CHIP COOKIE

BIG-TIME, HOMEMADE COOKIES, FULL OF CHOCOLATE CHUNKS AND CRUNCHY WALNUTS, WILL SATISFY THE WHOLE FAMILY.

1 cup packed brown sugar
¾ cup granulated sugar
1 cup margarine or butter, softened
1 teaspoon vanilla
2 eggs
2½ cups all-purpose flour
¾ teaspoon baking soda
¾ teaspoon salt
12 ounces semisweet or milk chocolate, coarsely chopped, or 2 cups semisweet chocolate chips
1 cup chopped walnuts

Heat oven to 375°. Beat sugars and margarine in large bowl on medium speed until fluffy, about 5 minutes. Beat in vanilla and eggs; beat in flour, baking soda and salt on low speed. Stir in chocolate and walnuts.

Drop dough by ¼ cupfuls about 2 inches apart onto ungreased cookie sheet; flatten slightly with fork. Bake until edges are light brown, 11 to 14 minutes. Let stand 3 to 4 minutes before removing from cookie sheet. Cool on wire rack.

18 cookies

SHERRIED BREAD PUDDING

A STOUT AND COMFORTING DESSERT CONJURES UP IMAGES OF COZY CHAIRS AND FIRESIDE CHATS.

1¼ cups milk
¼ cup margarine or butter
2 eggs, slightly beaten
¾ cup dried fruit snack mix (peaches, apricots, apples and raisins) or ½ cup cut-up dried mixed fruit and ¼ cup golden raisins
½ cup sugar
⅓ cup cream sherry or sweet red wine
½ teaspoon ground nutmeg
¼ teaspoon salt
4 cups 1-inch French bread cubes (about 5 slices)
Sherry Cream (below)

Heat oven to 350°. Heat milk and margarine over medium heat until margarine is melted and milk is scalded. Mix eggs, snack mix, sugar, sherry, nutmeg and salt in ungreased 1½-quart casserole; stir in bread cubes. Pour in milk mixture. Place casserole in pan of very hot water (1 inch deep).

Bake uncovered until knife inserted 1 inch from edge of casserole comes out clean, 40 to 45 minutes. Serve warm with Sherry Cream.

8 servings

SHERRY CREAM

½ cup whipping cream
1 tablespoon cream sherry or sweet red wine

Beat whipping cream in chilled small bowl until stiff. Gently stir in sherry.

SWEET RICE WITH CINNAMON

POWDERED SUGAR DISAPPEARS BEAUTIFULLY INTO GRAINS OF WHITE RICE TO SWEETEN THIS MOROCCAN DISH. CINNAMON ADDS A WARM TOUCH.

1⅓ cups regular rice
2⅔ cups water
½ teaspoon salt
¼ cup margarine or butter
¼ cup powdered sugar
Ground cinnamon

Heat rice, water and salt to boiling in 3-quart saucepan, stirring once or twice; reduce heat. Cover and simmer 14 minutes. (Do not lift cover or stir.) Remove from heat. Fluff rice lightly with fork; cover and let steam 5 to 10 minutes. Stir in margarine and powdered sugar. Sprinkle with cinnamon; serve warm.

6 servings

CRUNCHY PUMPKIN MOUSSE

SMOOTH SOFT MOUSSE PROVIDES WONDERFUL CONTRAST TO THE CRISP CRUNCHY TEXTURE OF HAZELNUT BUTTER CRUNCH.

Hazelnut Butter Crunch (right)
2 teaspoons unflavored gelatin
¼ cup cold water
¾ cup canned pumpkin
⅓ cup packed brown sugar
¼ teaspoon each salt, ground ginger, ground cinnamon and ground nutmeg
2 eggs, separated
½ cup chilled whipping cream
¼ teaspoon cream of tartar
⅓ cup granulated sugar
Sweetened Whipped Cream (right)

Prepare Hazelnut Butter Crunch. Sprinkle gelatin on cold water in 1-quart saucepan to soften; heat over medium heat, stirring constantly, until gelatin is dissolved. Stir in pumpkin, brown sugar, salt, spices and egg yolks. Heat just to boiling over medium heat, stirring constantly. Refrigerate, stirring occasionally, until mixture mounds slightly when dropped from a spoon, about 15 minutes.

Beat whipping cream in chilled bowl until soft peaks form; beat in cooled pumpkin mixture, ⅓ at a time, until well blended.

Beat egg whites and cream of tartar in small bowl until foamy. Beat in ⅓ cup granulated sugar, 1 tablespoon at a time, until stiff and glossy. (Do not underbeat.) Fold pumpkin mixture into egg white mixture.

Spoon 2 tablespoons Hazelnut Butter Crunch into each of 5 sherbet dishes; top with ½ cup pumpkin mixture. Top with 2 tablespoons Hazelnut Butter Crunch. Refrigerate until set, 2 to 3 hours.

Top each dish with whipped cream just before serving. Garnish with hazelnuts or crystallized ginger if desired. Refrigerate any remaining desserts.

5 servings

HAZELNUT BUTTER CRUNCH

½ cup all-purpose flour
⅓ cup chopped hazelnuts (see page 25)
¼ cup packed brown sugar
¼ cup margarine or butter

Heat oven to 400°. Mix all ingredients until crumbly. Distribute evenly in ungreased, rectangular pan, 13 x 9 x 2 inches. Bake until golden brown, 7 to 10 minutes; stir and cool. Store covered until ready to use, up to 2 days.

SWEETENED WHIPPED CREAM

¾ cup chilled whipping cream
2 tablespoons granulated or powdered sugar

Beat all ingredients in a chilled bowl until stiff.

FRESH FRUIT TOSTADAS

Tostada Shells (below)
1 can (17 ounces) apricot halves, drained
2 tablespoons honey
1 cup strawberry halves
1 cup sliced peaches or apricots
1 cup quartered fresh figs or plums
½ cup whipping cream
2 tablespoons powdered sugar

Prepare Tostada Shells. Place apricot halves and honey in food processor workbowl fitted with steel blade or in blender container; cover and process until smooth.

Mix apricot mixture, strawberries, peaches and fig. Spoon about ½ cup mixture into each tostada shell.

Beat whipping cream and powdered sugar in chilled bowl until stiff. Serve with tostadas.

6 servings

TOSTADA SHELLS

6 flour tortillas (6 to 7 inches in diameter), warmed
Margarine or butter, softened
½ cup semisweet chocolate chips
1 teaspoon shortening

Heat oven to 400°. Spread one side of each tortilla with margarine. Press each tortilla, margarine side down, in ungreased 10-ounce custard cup. Place custard cups in jelly roll pan, 15½ x 10½ x 1 inch. Bake until light golden brown, about 10 minutes. Remove shells from custard cups. Heat chocolate chips and shortening until melted; drizzle over insides of tostada shells. If necessary, refrigerate until chocolate is firm, 3 to 4 minutes.

Berry Pirouette

BERRY PIROUETTE

YOU MAY SUBSTITUTE BLUEBERRIES FOR BOYSENBERRIES IN THIS SPECTACULAR, DO-AHEAD DESSERT.

1¾ cups boiling water
2 packages (3 ounces each) raspberry-flavored gelatin
1 package (16 ounces) frozen boysenberries, partially thawed
2 cups chilled whipping cream
1 package (5½ ounces) tube-shaped pirouette cookies (about 24)

Pour boiling water on gelatin in large bowl; stir until gelatin is dissolved. Reserve 3 to 5 berries for garnish. Place remaining berries in food processor workbowl fitted with steel blade or in blender container. Cover and process until smooth. Stir berries into gelatin. Refrigerate until very thick but not set, about 1 hour.

Beat gelatin mixture on high speed until thick and fluffy, about 4 minutes. Beat 1 cup of the whipping cream in chilled bowl until stiff; fold into gelatin mixture. Pour into springform pan, 9 x 3 inches. Refrigerate until set, about 3 hours.

Run knife around edge of dessert to loosen; remove side of pan. Place dessert on serving plate. Beat remaining 1 cup whipping cream in chilled bowl until stiff. Spread side of dessert with half of the whipped cream.

Carefully cut cookies crosswise into halves. Arrange cookies, cut sides down, vertically around side of dessert; press lightly. Garnish with remaining whipped cream and berries.

10 to 12 servings

PEACH PIROUETTE: Substitute 1 package (16 ounces) frozen sliced peaches, partially thawed, for the boysenberries and orange-flavored gelatin for the raspberry-flavored gelatin. Reserve 3 peach slices for garnish.

TUCSON LEMON CAKE

ARIZONA LOVES LEMON AND GROWS ITS OWN IN PROFUSION.

1½ cups sugar
½ cup margarine or butter, softened
3 eggs
2½ cups all-purpose flour
1 teaspoon baking soda
½ teaspoon salt
1 cup buttermilk
¼ cup poppy seed
2 tablespoons grated lemon peel
2 tablespoons lemon juice
Lemon Glaze (below)

Heat oven to 325°. Grease and flour 12-cup bundt cake pan or tube pan, 10 x 4 inches. Beat sugar and margarine in large bowl on medium speed until light and fluffy. Beat in eggs, 1 at a time.

Mix flour, baking soda and salt; beat into sugar mixture alternately with buttermilk until well blended. Stir in poppy seed, lemon peel and lemon juice. Spread in pan.

Bake until wooden pick inserted in center comes out clean, 50 to 55 minutes. Immediately poke holes in top of cake with long-tined fork; pour about ⅔ of the Lemon Glaze over top. Cool 20 minutes. Invert on heatproof serving plate; remove pan. Spread with remaining glaze.

16 servings

LEMON GLAZE

2 cups powdered sugar
¼ cup margarine or butter, melted
2 tablespoons grated lemon peel
¼ cup lemon juice

Mix all ingredients.

DATE-PECAN UPSIDE-DOWN CAKE

¼ cup plus 2 tablespoons margarine or butter
⅔ cup packed brown sugar
12 pitted dates
1 cup coarsely chopped pecans
1 cup all-purpose flour
¾ cup granulated sugar
⅓ cup shortening
¾ cup milk
1½ teaspoons baking powder
1 teaspoon vanilla
½ teaspoon salt
1 egg
Whipped cream

Heat oven to 350°. Heat margarine in 10-inch ovenproof skillet or square pan, 9 x 9 x 2 inches, in oven until melted. Sprinkle evenly with brown sugar. Arrange dates on top so that each serving will include one date; sprinkle with pecans.

Beat remaining ingredients except whipped cream in large bowl on low speed, scraping bowl constantly, 30 seconds. Beat on high speed, scraping bowl occasionally, 3 minutes. Pour evenly over dates and pecans.

Bake until wooden pick inserted in center comes out clean, 40 to 45 minutes. Loosen edge of cake with knife. Invert on heatproof platter; leave skillet over cake a few minutes. Serve warm with whipped cream.

12 servings

Tucson Lemon Cake

GARDEN APPLE ICE CREAM

HERE IS A LOVELY AND SENTIMENTAL ENGLISH DESSERT. A TOUCH OF ROSE WATER ADDS THE ESSENCE OF WARM-WEATHER BLOSSOMS. SERVE THIS ICE CREAM WITH THIN WAFER COOKIES.

3 egg yolks, beaten
½ cup sugar
½ cup milk
¼ teaspoon salt
2 cups chilled whipping cream
¾ cup frozen apple juice concentrate, thawed (6 ounces)
½ to 1 teaspoon rose water
3 to 4 drops red food color (optional)

Mix egg yolks, sugar, milk and salt in 2-quart saucepan. Cook over medium heat, stirring constantly, just until bubbles appear around edge. Pour into chilled bowl; cover and refrigerate until room temperature, 1 to 2 hours.

Stir remaining ingredients into milk mixture. Pour into freezer can; put dasher in place. Cover and adjust crank. Place can in freezer tub. Fill freezer tub ⅓ full of ice; add remaining ice alternately with layers of rock salt (6 parts ice to 1 part rock salt). Turn crank until it turns with difficulty. Drain water from freezer tub. Remove lid; take out dasher. Pack mixture down; replace lid. Repack in ice and salt. Let stand several hours to ripen.

8 servings

Garden Apple Ice Cream

ROSE WATER

It is the influence of India and the Middle East that has made rose water known throughout the culinary world. This clear liquid, distilled from fresh rose petals, is a flavoring that can be subtle and romantic when used judiciously, soapy when added with a heavy hand. Rose essence, a more concentrated form of rose flavoring, should be added more sparingly to dishes than rose water.

MANGO-HONEY ICE CREAM

HERE IS A LUSCIOUS, SWEET COMBINATION THAT COULD ONLY BE HOMEMADE: CREAM, HONEY, MANGO AND CINNAMON.

2 eggs
¾ cup sugar
½ cup milk
2 tablespoons honey
½ teaspoon ground cinnamon
¼ teaspoon salt
2 cups whipping cream
½ teaspoon vanilla
3 cans (15 ounces each) sliced mangoes (see page 7), drained and mashed

Beat eggs in 2-quart saucepan; mix in sugar, milk, honey, cinnamon and salt. Heat just to simmering over medium heat, stirring constantly. Cool to room temperature. Stir in whipping cream, vanilla and mangoes. Freeze according to ice cream maker manufacturer's directions.

8 servings

APPENDIX

Set aside at least one day each month to serve a truly special meal to family or friends. Here are some menu suggestions for the year-round.

MENUS

(ASTERISK INDICATES RECIPE INCLUDED)

JANUARY

Southwest Sautéed Scallops*
Fettuccine
Mixed Green Salad
Hard Rolls
Tuscon Lemon Cake*

FEBRUARY

Seafood Chilaquiles Casserole*
Vegetable Cornmeal Muffins*
Radish and Watercress Salad*
Mango-Honey Ice Cream*

MARCH

Chorizo-stuffed Beef Roast*
Hearts of Palm in Tomato Sauce*
Baked Plantains*
Rice with Chayote*
Tropical Fruit with Chocolate Sauce*

APRIL

Salmon with Cucumber Salsa*
Lemon and Celery Pilaf*
Bran-Sunflower Nut Bread*
Brown Sugar Pear Tart*

MAY

Moroccan Chicken with Olives*
Sweet Rice with Cinnamon*
Tomatoes, Peppers and Onions*
Fruit Sorbet

JUNE

Grilled Red Snapper with Vegetable Sauté*
Texas Slaw with Cumin Dressing*
Adobe Bread*
Peach Cobbler with Caramel Sauce*

JULY

Mexican Grilled Steak*
Grilled Corn with Chile-Lime Spread*
Jicama Citrus Salad with Sangria Dressing*
Flour Tortillas
Date-Pecan Upside-down Cake*

AUGUST

Pasta with Vegetable and Goat Cheese Sauce*
Italian Tomato and Bread Salad*
Prosciutto, Sun-dried Tomato and Basil Muffins*
Southwest Lemon Fruit Tart*

SEPTEMBER

Lamb Patties with Summer Squash*
Fresh Herb and Tomato Salad*
Pine Nut and Green Onion Pilaf*
French Bread
Crunchy Pumpkin Mousse*

OCTOBER

Peach-glazed Pork Roast*
Radish and Watercress Salad*
French Garden Peas*
Caramelized Sweet Potatoes*
Honey-Wine Cranberry Tart*

NOVEMBER

Butternut Squash Soup*
Company Pot Roast*
Steamed New Potatoes
Buttered Broccoli
Casserole Bread*
Garden Apple Ice Cream*

DECEMBER

Chicken with Lemon Grass*
Steamed Broccoli
Wild Rice
Oat-Peach Muffins*
Berry Pirouette*

INDEX

Credits

Vice President and Publisher: Anne M. Zeman

Senior Editor: Rebecca W. Atwater

Art Director: Laurence Alexander

Photographer: Nanci E. Doonan

Designer: Patricia Fabricant

Production Editor: John Paul Jones